What Other

"I laughed and cried reading this book. Yes, there is hope, there is second chance, there is recovery, and there is fullness of life. All we need is to surrender to Jesus. Sheryl's book is a book of hope. The transparency Sheryl uses is a true testimony of God's work to make a broken woman into a godly woman. Way to go Sheryl."

—**Dr. Laila Risgallah**, PhD
Founder and President
Not Guilty for Family Development

"Sheryl Giesbrecht shares honestly and powerfully how God strengthened her in the midst of a challenging life. Her genuine sharing and applicable ideas helped me to trust God more. I'm confident *Get Back Up* will be a gift of encouragement that will give you an 'I can do all things in Christ' kind of confidence. Open this book and open yourself to God's loving heart."

—**Kathy Collard Miller**
Speaker, Author of *Women of the Bible*

"If you are a child of God, you can be sure that trials are coming your way. If you need hands on, practical insight on what it looks like to get back on your feet, this book is a must-read. With transparency and vulnerability, Sheryl shows her readers how mightily God worked in the midst of her unimaginable trials."

—**Judy Hampton**
Speaker, Author of *When Your Plans Fall Through, Under the Circumstances,* and *Ready? Set? Go!*

"*Get Back Up* is a book for every woman who has ever wanted to overcome obstacles, live courageously, let go of grudges, pursue her dreams, and live a vibrant Christian life. Sheryl Giesbrecht has given us a resource that's filled with biblical truth, practical applications, poignant illustrations, and personal vulnerability. You'll want one copy for yourself and then you'll want to lead a small group through this life-changing study that includes thought-provoking questions after each chapter. *Get Back Up* will be one of your new favorites!"

—Carol Kent
Speaker, Author of *Becoming a Woman of Influence*

"This book of truths, stories, and practical pointers should be handed to every new Christian with a note that says: 'When you hit a wall (and you will), read this. Better yet, read it now!'"

—Jan Johnson
Author of *When the Soul Listens*
and *Enjoying the Presence of God*

"It's refreshing to read a book that captivates and holds your interest so well. It's easy to read, speaks to life's issues, and is highly practical. Sheryl's transparency as well as her dependency on God's word makes this a worthwhile resource."

—H. Norman Wright
Author, Marriage and Family Therapist

Get
Back
Up

Get

Trusting God When Life

Back

Knocks You Down

Up

Sheryl Giesbrecht

Get Back Up: Trusting God When Life Knocks You Down

Published by Wheatmark®
1760 East River Road, Suite 145
Tucson, Arizona 85718 U.S.A.
www.wheatmark.com

ISBN: 978-1-60494-854-7 (paperback)
ISBN: 978-1-60494-876-9 (ebook)
LCCN: 2012946146

rev201401

This book is dedicated for the glory of God,
that His name may be known
in every tribe, tongue, and nation.

*"Declare His glory among the nations, his marvelous deeds
among all peoples."* —Psalm 96:3 (NIV)

Acknowledgments

First and foremost, I thank God the Father for His love, His son Jesus Christ for His grace, and the Holy Spirit for His presence. My Lord taught me what it means to get back up. "Because of the Lord's love we are not consumed, for his compassions never fail. They are new every morning; great is your faithfulness. I say to myself, 'The Lord is my portion; therefore I will wait for Him.'" Lamentations 3:22-24 (NIV)

To mention those who have contributed to this book is to thank those who have mentored me spiritually. My mother, Shirley Adkins, whose example of daily, early morning Bible study and prayer provides a baseline for my regular routine. My late husband, Pastor Paul "Rock" Giesbrecht; my partner in over thirty years of ministry, including three pastorates and international travel, my best friend, speaking coach, and head cheerleader. My mother-in-law, Miriam Giesbrecht Robnett, who gave me a great gift early in my marriage and opened the door for me to sit at the feet of great Bible teachers – Jill Briscoe and Anne Graham Lotz. Pat Slagle, friend, confidant, prayer partner and counselor, who challenged me to seek "honey from the rock" in the midst of the darkest times. Carol Wilcox, friend, assistant, and editor, read between the lines of my life and manuscript as she helped me walk the road to complete this book.

The list of women influencers who invested a piece of themselves through wisdom, a listening ear, or a heartfelt prayer is near and dear to my heart. My sisters, Kathy Harrell and Becki Richter, along with my sisters-in-law, Yuriko Adkins, Sheryle Saunders, and Marlene Alvey continue to walk with me through the family ties we share. Other influencers include pastors, authors, speakers, and professors who taught me through written or spoken works. I thank God for my children, Sarah Giesbrecht Hunter and husband, Matt, and my son, Ben Thomas Giesbrecht, and wife, Megan.

All My Love and Thanks to My Heavenly Father.

—Sheryl Giesbrecht

"Since my youth, O God, you have taught me, and to this day I declare your marvelous deeds. Even when I am old and gray, do not forsake me O God, till I declare your power to the next generation, your might to all who are to come. Your righteousness reaches to the skies, O God, you, who have done great things. Who, O God, is like you? Though you have made me see troubles, many and bitter, you will restore my life again; from the depths of the earth, you again will bring me up."

—Psalm 71:17-20 (NIV)

Contents

Foreword by Pam Farrel xiii

Foreword by Dr. Neil T. Anderson xix

Chapter Summaries xxiii

1   Take My Hand 1

2   Grab onto Truth 13

In Christ I Am: Bookmark 27

3   Let Grudges Go 31

4   Hanging by a Thread. 47

5   Alone and Afraid 59

6   Leveled by Loneliness......................73

7   Piled in a Heap...........................87

8   Tripped up over Technology 99

9   Flat on My Face 111

10   Rise and Shine 121

Endnotes......................................135

God Thoughts: Experiencing Him by His Names.......141

Foreword

By Pam Farrel

Sheryl Giesbrecht defines the word "overcomer." I have watched her resilient spirit over the years of our friendship. It was our heart to help others overcome that first connected our lives in ministry. We are so kindred of heart that when God called us to a new ministry post, He answered our prayers for a Christian family to buy our home by having Sheryl and her husband buy the home we had just remodeled! The Giesbrechts continued to hold up the light of God's love in that community in spite of numerous obstacles. Sheryl's "with God, all things are possible" attitude has inspired a city then, but now people around the world are impacted by her wise words of faith and lifestyle of acting on the beliefs she holds dear.

In my book, *Becoming a Brave New Woman* I write, "Show me the size of your God, I will show you the size of your adventure. Big God—Big adventure! Show me the size of your God, I will show you the size of your courage. Big

God—Big courage!" Based upon the courage Sheryl writes about in this book, she has a VERY BIG GOD! And she wants you to experience the power, provision and peace that a big God can bring to your life, too!

Sheryl's life is inspiring. She owns the ability to face down and hurdle over traumas that would cause most women to curl up in a ball, pull up the covers and eat a gallon of chocolate chip cookie dough ice cream! And she even handles life's storms with a good sense of humor. In my book, *10 Secrets of Living Strong, Smart and Savvy*, I use Sheryl as a great example of how to "choose joy" no matter what life sends your way.

Sheryl was diagnosed with an aggressive form of cancer. She immediately turned to God for help and strength. She meditated on verses like, "My body and mind may grow weak, He is my strength, all I ever need." (Psalm 73:26) . . . Sheryl then began to anticipate how God was going to turn the dark cloud inside out so she could see the silver lining. With that choice, hope pushed its bright ray through the darkness. Sheryl writes this about her chemotherapy:

> We developed our sense of humor to include "tumor humor" – the chemotherapy was cutting edge, only on the market three years and was made of mouse protein. So we developed our own mouse jokes. During the first treatment, I had developed a reaction to the medication. I told the nurse "I had this unusual craving to build a nest and eat cheese." He said "I think your tail was trying to grow too fast." I now have all kinds of mouse stuff; my sister-in-law even gave us a pair of Mickey Mouse ears."

I am excited for each of you who will read this book because I have been praying with Sheryl for over twenty years that the book she carried in her heart would one day make it into print. She has always held in her heart the desire to encourage, empower, and enlighten women with the tools to gain victory and move into the "future and hope" that God promises. And she never gives up until she sees God accomplish His promises! Because of her tenacity, you and I are blessed by her words and example.

My first book is entitled *Woman of Influence: 10 Traits of Those Who Want to Make a Difference.* And when I look at all the qualities needed to be a woman of influence and impact, Sheryl has them all—especially the ability to grasp an accurate picture of who God is, and then live as if she believed every word God said about Himself and His ability to handle life. God is called mighty, and Sheryl lives 100 percent in God's might. Mighty in the Old Testament is often linked to meaning firm, strong, or showing power or force. It is the kind of power that many would perceive as miraculous. When used of God, one could say HE MAKES courage; when used of us, we could say we TAKE courage. God can be the source or provider of the might, strength, or power we need.

Moses talks of God's mighty hand frequently, for example, Exodus 13:14 (NIV):

In days to come, when your son asks you, "What does this mean?" say to him, "With a mighty hand the Lord brought us out of Egypt, out of the land of slavery."

There is a sense we are to stand in awe of God's mighty power because it is overwhelmingly better, far superior to even the mightiest, fiercest, toughest warrior. And many times as I have seen God be mighty in Sheryl's life I have stood in awe. Deuteronomy 3:24 (NIV) reminds:

> *Sovereign* LORD, *you have begun to show to your servant your greatness and your strong hand. For what god is there in heaven or on earth who can do the deeds and mighty works you do?*

(The answer to this question is NO ONE can compare with God's mighty power).

Sometimes I think we do not see this mighty hand of God because we live too safe, too reliant on our own abilities. To really see God's power, we need to get out on the edge, out on the limb, out of our comfort zone. We need to truly TRUST God. Sheryl lives out on the edge of life where God must show up to make life work. She models this kind of powerful trust in a mighty God. Sheryl will help you gain that kind of trust so that no matter what life sends your way, you will have the tools, the heart, the wisdom, and the will to get back up holding on to God's mighty hand.

What are you believing God for? Where do you need His mighty power to show up? Life might knock you down, but God will pick you up—if you hold onto His mighty hand.

I have placed this verse on my bathroom mirror—it has

helped empower my belief in God's power to pick me back up:

> *...the God of our Lord Jesus Christ, the Father of glory, may give to you the spirit of wisdom and revelation in the knowledge of Him, 18 the eyes of your understanding being enlightened; that you may know what is the hope of His calling, what are the riches of the glory of His inheritance in the saints, 19 and what is the exceeding greatness of His power toward us who believe, **according to the working of His mighty power** 20 which He worked in Christ when He raised Him from the dead and seated Him at His right hand in the heavenly places ...*
> (Eph 1:17–20 NKJV emphasis added)

The same power that raised Christ can raise your hope today! Sheryl believes this, Sheryl lives this, Sheryl models this, and in this book, Sheryl brings to life how you can see this same mighty God work in your life too. God will use the words on these pages to gather you up in His arms, shelter you, feed you wisdom through the scenes of Sheryl's life, and then He will help you stand, and stand strong. He did it for Sheryl. He did it for me. God will do it for you!

• •

Pam Farrel is the author of over thirty-eight books including best-selling Men Are Like Waffles, Women Are Like Spaghetti, 10 Best Decisions a Woman Can Make, *international speaker, and co-director of Love-Wise Ministry (www.Love-Wise.com)*

Foreword

By Dr. Neil T. Anderson

"Who are you?" Nothing more personal could ever be asked, and few can give a substantive answer. Thales of Miletus, considered one of the wise men of Greece, lived five centuries before Christ. When asked, "What is most difficult?" He replied, "To know thyself."

How would you answer that question? Would you give your name? Your nationality? Your vocation? Several hundred average people were asked that question on the streets and in their work places. It was an informal study conducted by psychologists. Most were startled by the question, and didn't know how to respond. Some got defensive, while others described their character, family, or job. One man answered, "Why I don't know; I have never been asked that question before."

I wasn't in ministry very long before I noticed that most people don't inherently feel good about themselves. Becoming a Christian didn't necessarily change their self-perception. So I read some psychological books on self-esteem that were woefully inadequate to explain the essence of our being. Social scientists have probed deeper into the subconscious than ever before, but as to the question of who we are, they have only scratched the surface. Secularists can provide a psychological profile of your personality, but that is very different from the essence of who we are as human beings created in the image of God.

Self-help psychology may lead to some form of self-actualization, but it ends with mere humanity trying to make a name for themselves, which will soon fade in time. Stroking one another's egos and picking yourself up by your own effort has no lasting effect on one's self-perception. The world looks for social status, exemplary performance, or appearance to be somebody of worth, but that always crumples under hostile rejection or morbid introspection.

I was searching for answers myself when God called me out of the pastorate to teach at Talbot School of Theology. It was in my second year of teaching that I discovered who I was in Christ. I may have known that theologically, but now I knew internally and eternally in a way that only God can make happen. Then I observed that every defeated Christian that I was trying to help had one thing in common. None of them knew who they were in Christ, nor did they understand what it meant to be a child of God. If the Holy Spirit is bearing witness with our spirit that we are children of God (Rom. 8:16), why weren't they sensing that? The apostle John wrote,

"But to all who did receive Him, who believed in His name, he gave the right to become children of God" (Jn. 1:12). Why doesn't every believer know that?

Knowing who I am in Christ was my anchor for the coming storm, which I share in my memoirs (*Rough Road to Freedom*, Hudson Lion, 2012). First, my wife became deathly ill and I wasn't sure she was going to survive. We lost our home and all our life savings paying medical expenses. Then my 15-year-old daughter was raped by two high school boys. God brought me to the end of my resources so that I could discover His. Every book that I have written, every tape that I have recorded, and every video shot was all after this "magnificent defeat" of self sufficiency. Freedom in Christ Ministries was born out of brokenness, and so was this book you are now reading.

Like myself, Sheryl did not sign up for martyrdom. We were hoping for an easier road, but we were led down *the road less chosen*. Not too many were standing by the wayside cheering us on, but there was One who promised to never leave nor forsake us. There may be a swamp in your path of uncertain destination. This book will help you navigate your way through. Those who endure to the end will be liberated children of God, anchored into the eternal streams of God's kingdom, and equipped to help others survive the storms of life.

Neither my wife, Joanne, myself, nor Sheryl knew fully what we signed up for when we made that commitment to full-time Christian service. If we had looked through the window of time and saw what we and our families would have to go through, we may not have come. But looking back, we are glad that we came. God's will is good, acceptable, and perfect.

• •

Dr. Neil T. Anderson is Founder and President Emeritus of Freedom in Christ Ministries

Chapter Summaries

Chapter 1: Take My Hand

Today's woman needs to know and respond to God's offer of a life worth living. His invitation extends to everyone. After years of independence and feeling overlooked as she watched others, author Sheryl Giesbrecht found true love when she accepted God's request. As a young girl, Giesbrecht dreamed of growing up to marry a prince, but early rejection and teen pressures to experiment with drugs and alcohol nearly sidetracked that dream until God stepped in with His invitation. Now she wants all women to accept that same invitation and let God hold them close in a grace-filled, guilt-free embrace. Accepting the invitation is the only way to *Get Back Up*.

Chapter 2: Grab onto Truth

Women find their true identities when they understand and believe what God thinks and how He sees them. Women's minds are programmed, often at an early age, to try to fix themselves or be like someone else. Giesbrecht uses her story of adjustment to life as a newlywed, relocation to an undesirable city, and explains her journey to discovery. She shows personal examples of surrender, explains applications for identity in Christ, and offers tips for transformation to maintain freedom.

Chapter 3: Let Grudges Go

Every day, women are given opportunities to offer forgiveness. Circumstances require us to give up our grudges, whether the offense is small, such as being gossiped about or lied to, or large, such as being robbed or hit by a drunk driver. Giesbrecht's pastor-husband was fired from his church position for no biblical or ethical reason. She found freedom through forgiveness. God ushered her into a deeper walk with Him through this step of trust.

Chapter 4: Hanging by a Thread

Finding balance in life is difficult as women juggle their diverse roles. Giesbrecht's fairytale life wasn't at all what she thought it would be. Her preschool children had multiple health issues. She was a worn-out, working mother and pastor's wife spread thin by a demanding college and singles' ministry. It seemed there was no time for herself— until she discovered the rejuvenating power of prayer through praise, meditation, intercession, and Bible study.

Chapter 5: Alone and Afraid

Do you ever feel alone trying to keep up with the hectic pace of life? Women often experience isolation during times of stress: family alcoholism, parental and spousal divorce, and even insensitive church members and pastoral staff can all take a toll. There was a time when Giesbrecht felt abandoned as a wife, mother, and servant of God. Through this season of loneliness, God made it clear that, although Giesbrecht felt lonely, she would never be alone. He would always be there for her.

Chapter 6: Leveled by Loneliness

Friends are important in every woman's life. Each season of change can be one of growth when a woman shares it with a girlfriend. Godly female friends are especially important during transitions such as a move or unexpected event. Women understand other women and provide emotional strength to make adjustments. Giesbrecht describes how she took a risk and reached out to make a friend with another woman. She shows how she trusted God in her fear of friendship and allowed God to fill her with more of Him.

Chapter 7: Piled in a Heap

During change, women must learn to flex or they will break. Each transition brings an opportunity to trust, even though our emotions may take a beating. Giesbrecht describes a six-month period of adjustment, during which her husband moved to a new job, one of her children transferred to a different school, and a family member had a serious accident. She learned to rely on God and His stability in the midst of her life modifications. Giesbrecht experienced firsthand His faithfulness, goodness, and provision.

Chapter 8: Tripped up over Technology

In many households, women filter what is watched on television and on the computer. Unfortunately, Internet pornography is easily accessible for the person who is needy, lonely, overwhelmed, or just plain bored. The author shares her husband's own struggle with and victory against Internet pornography, its effects on their marriage and ministry, and how God healed them through the crisis.

Chapter 9: Flat on My Face

Most women today know how to perform regular breast self-examinations as a preventative measure, but no woman ever expects to find a lump. Giesbrecht describes the lessons she learned when she found a lump under her eye that was diagnosed as cancer. She discusses the struggles of receiving diagnosis, treatment, and recovery from cancer—and she talks about the joys of being healed from a life-threatening disease and her life as a victorious cancer survivor.

Chapter 10: Rise and Shine

Death's interruption is usually unwelcome, especially if it's the loss of a spouse. Women want to know how to rejoice in the midst of unthinkable tragedy. Giesbrecht's husband was killed in a tragic motorcycle accident. Her plans, dreams, and hopes for the future were suddenly rearranged. She found courage, confidence, and joy as she walked through the "valley of the shadow of death." God wants nothing more than for us to experience His love, presence, power, and peace, even when we don't understand or appreciate His will.

1

Take My Hand

Is it possible to survive a free-fall from the Sears Tower in Chicago? The answer is yes. What if on your vacation you slipped off the tenth-floor balcony of your hotel? Would you live to mentally replay the saga? Or when you fulfill a lifelong dream of skydiving and your parachute fails, could you survive the fall? The answer is still yes. The Wiki How-To manual says, "Hundreds, maybe thousands of people have fallen from such heights and lived to tell the tale."[1]

Perhaps you are thinking: *This could never happen to me; I will never visit Chicago; I don't stay in hotels with more than three floors; and, furthermore, I will never skydive.* So what does this have to do with you and me? These stories seem like extreme examples of a tragic plunge to almost certain catastrophe. Believe it or not, one can increase chances of survival by merely putting to use a few helpful skills.

Remember skinned knees and bruised elbows? Chalk up these casualties to part of the process when you learned to ride a bike or roller skate. You probably went down hard the first few times you fell, but after that, you learned to anticipate how to avoid the fall and planned ahead a little better. Once you applied learned techniques, common sense, and God-given intuition, you avoided falling again. We literally trip and fall as we walk through life, like toddlers who move from cruising the couch to the first wobbly steps on their own, but then—whoops!—land face-first on the floor. Adults unfortunately fall too. Picture the one enthusiastic shopper who rushes to the cash register with an armload of must-have sale items. The leather soles of her boots hit the freshly waxed floor and, as if she's stepped on a skateboard, her feet slip out from under her. The woman tries to break her fall with her hands and turns loose the sale items, which sail into orbit overhead. Surprised and embarrassed, the woman lands posterior down and feet up, the items falling nearby. Stunned, she looks around. Things she had to have but now could leave behind surround her. Accidental bodily falls are just that: they happen when we least expect them and leave us surrounded by a mess.

Beyond the literal, physical ways we trip, teeter, or collapse, life brings change and challenges that can move us out of our comfort zones. Facing emotional, spiritual, or physical challenges can plunge us into aimless descent. Ever felt like you've been tripped up by an addiction? Maybe you've been tormented by shame? Slipped up by doubt? Or fallen headlong into depression? God is near and waits for us to ask Him to help us get back up when we are knocked down by life into a downward spiral, even if we splatter on the sidewalk. God wants us to reach out to Him in times of difficulty, doubt, despair, depression, disappointment, disease, destruction, divorce, discouragement, domestic violence, or death. God's hand is extended to us. His will for us when we are down and out is to turn to Him and ask for a hand up. He asks us to lace our fingers into His. "God gives a hand to those down on their luck, gives a fresh start to those ready to quit" (Psalm 145:14 [*The Message*]).

Off the Edge

There was a time in my life when I fell hard. I was an angry sixteen-year-old alcoholic, drug addict, and in trouble with the law. Loving parents raised me in a Christian home; yet I questioned God's love. One night my friends and I were partying in a remote area, drinking beer, and smoking dope. We heard the siren before we saw the patrol car's approaching headlights. We couldn't get away. The officer ordered us to get out of our vehicle, and we were thoroughly searched. Most of my friends were minors breaking curfew and not of legal drinking age. The sheriff gave them warning citations and sent them home. I was arrested.

Handcuffed in the back seat of the sheriff's patrol car, I couldn't believe I was the only one to be arrested. *Where were my friends? Why did they desert me? Why did they pin the guilt on me? Why weren't they there for me?* I felt abandoned, alone, and abused. I was checked into the detention facility; my purse and clothes were taken away. I was told to put on a uniform: stiff elastic-waist pants and a scratchy orange sweater. This had to be a bad dream.

A few hours later, I woke up. The cot beneath me felt stone cold to my touch; the cement ceiling above seemed stark, haunting, and crushing. I realized these confines were not my bedroom. I turned on my side and sat up. My head spun. I stood up on quivering legs, looked straight ahead, and saw a barred steel door. I recalled the night before: I had been arrested. This was not a dream; it was a nightmare—and it was real.

I ran to the steel door, grabbed the bars on the window, and yelled, "I didn't do anything wrong! I don't deserve to be here!" I yelled and shook the bars, trying to open the steel door, but no one paid attention. I ran in circles like a caged animal, cussing, crying, and screaming. My mind flashed back to the time my desire for romantic love began. I was six years old. It was the end of kindergarten, and my teacher had awarded me the book *Sleeping Beauty* for perfect attendance. That summer I escaped for hours at a time into Princess Aurora's fairytale life. I imagined my hair long and blonde like hers, my life adventuresome— rescued by a handsome young prince whose kiss of true love would break the spell of ordinary life.

My mind was filled with longings from this early inno- cent age for a love that would hold me close through life. I dreamt of *the* one and only, *my* handsome prince who would sweep me off my feet, rescue me from my prob- lems, and fix all the broken and bruised places in my life. I was thinking of a man, not God. I hoped someday my dreams would come true and end as fairytales do—happily ever after.

My mind fast-forwarded to more recent junior high memories, my friends asking if I was going out, but I wasn't sure. I'd been out only one other time, to a dance at my school, and it had been a big disappointment. I'd watched the popular and handsome Dale from across the room, where he seemed to be looking at me, but then invited someone else to dance with him. I watched him walk away as my heart sank. *Will I be a wallflower my whole life?* I shuddered at the thought. The most important issue in my mind was the invitation, being asked. I wanted to be wanted. I decided to accept my friends' suggestion in the end and go to another dance. And I was rejected, again.

These painful memories added to my rage in the jail cell that day. There was no handsome prince to rescue me. No one cared. Exhausted and hung over, I melted into a sobbing heap in the middle of the cement floor and cried out, "God, if you're real, hear my prayer. Rescue me, save me, help me." God then began to draw me to Himself. Though I had fallen hard, I had not yet reached the bottom of the pit. I had asked for God's help, but I was holding back. Part of me still wanted my own way.

The Invitation

I was released from the detention facility, but the pattern of my choices repeated: I had more clashes with the law. Counseling, under the watch of a probation officer, a juvenile advocate, and attempts at rehabilitation were futile. Now seventeen, I was careening deeper into drug addiction. I stayed high as much as possible, trying to fill the emptiness in my life with the highest high or the cutest guy while my need for affection only increased. I couldn't wait to move out of my parents' home. My family pulled strings to get me a volunteer summer job at a Christian camp. The staff assigned me lists of chores, such as wash-

ing hundreds of dishes in the mess hall, raking piles of
pine needles around the campgrounds, and even moving
logs around the outdoor campfire ring.

Whenever I complained or threw fits over doing my
chores or smoked cigarettes and dope, the staff said, "Love
covers over a multitude of sins." (I Peter 4:8 [NIV]) Their
words, repeated over and over, immersed me for two
weeks. The staff didn't tell me to change anything about
my appearance, attitude, or addictions. Instead, they
showed me what the invitation of love looked like. They
were kind; they offered the true love of God without forcing me to accept it.

It got me to thinking, *Isn't my sin too much for God to
handle?*

That thought plagued me day and night. Their words,
"Love covers a multitude of sins," taken straight from scripture, began to penetrate my hard heart and foggy mind. I
began to believe God's love could cover the things that held
me captive to my addictions: drugs and alcohol, lying and
stealing, promiscuity and drug dealing. It was finally clear:
I didn't need to clean up my act before coming to God; He
loved me passionately just the way I was. One night in my
cabin, I submitted to the overwhelming love of God. He
had reached out to me, and I, a most unlikely choice, finally
grasped His hand. *His abundant love did cover my multitude
of sins.* I accepted the invitation to live a new life. It didn't
come from a boy. This invitation was from God.

May I Have Your Hand?

God loves us. God's love is true love. The real, tangible love of God is extravagant, passionate, and immeasurable. Brennan Manning said, "Trying to explain the love of God is like trying to contain the Gulf of Mexico in a shot glass."[2] God has loved us since the beginning of time. He draws us to Himself with a love that never fails, always hopes and wants the best for us. He asked His Son Jesus Christ to die in our place. Jesus was the acceptable sacrifice for our sins. "This is how God showed his love among us: he sent his one and only Son into the world that we might live through him. This is love: not that we loved God, but that he loved us and sent his Son as an atoning sacrifice for our sins" (I John 4:9–10 [NIV]).

Falling over hurts, habits, and hang-ups in life can draw you closer to God. Or you can resist His help, ignore His outstretched hand, and keep Him at a distance. What would it mean for you to accept His invitation and take His hand? God extends this invitation to a new life with true love (Jesus Christ) to everyone. Some women never accept it. But it doesn't have to be that way. Please listen. God wants to hold you close in a grace-filled, guilt-free embrace as you grasp His hand and walk together with Him through life.

Life to the Full

Once you've accepted His invitation, it's helpful to remember that old hurts, habits, and hang-ups don't just disappear. The imaginations of the enemy can try to haunt us. But God's love pays no account to our past sins. He's forgiven us of every one of them, and his love brings out the best in us. He wants us to respond to this love and believe that by faith He will use our past to His glory. "Even from my sins God has drawn good," said St. Augustine of Hippo.[3] Keep walking with God, trusting Him for each day's needs, and resting in His mighty arms. His is an everlasting gentle grip of grace. Learn to let Him lead. Moving in cadence with His steps will come. God's handbook, the Bible, is your instruction manual.

God loves to love us; we are always on His mind. We are His delight. God takes great pleasure in us. He has made us to love; that's our purpose. He is thrilled with us and wants us to be thrilled with Him. That's why He offers the invitation. What gives you joy? Whatever it is, that is your delight. According to *Webster's Dictionary*, to delight in something or someone means "to enjoy, to appreciate or to savor."[4] Delight in God, praise Him with a grateful heart, and thank Him for everything, even your pain. Choose to thank God, praise Him even for the circumstances you cannot change; it sets the stage for your new life.

Get up and take His hand. It's a choice to realize God's truth that you are loved, safe, and important. God's love mobilizes you to be all He has created you to be. Christ's love guarantees safety in your position in Christ; nothing and no one can remove you from the palm of His hand. God has an important plan for you in the kingdom. God has granted you divine favor through Christ's finished work on the cross; He died for you, was buried, and raised from the dead. An abundant life offered through Jesus Christ is lived in God's grace.

Vickie's Story

Vickie found strength to stand. Her first marriage ended with divorce. Her ex-husband was awarded custody of their children. She was lonely most of the time, and her heart was broken. She succumbed to a heap of depression, raising her head up only to watch life and happiness elude her. Vickie married again after a couple of years and was eventually diagnosed with breast cancer, which required chemotherapy. Down lower than ever before, she had forgotten how to get back up. Vickie and I met in a prayer group. She remembers:

The first time I heard Sheryl speak, it changed my thinking and my life. I felt God speaking to me. As Sheryl shared her past I felt like crying, because I realized there were things in my life that I had hidden. I did confess my sins to God, but something was not complete. Even though my sins were forgiven, I had not forgiven myself. When I forgave myself, I truly understood what Jesus did at the cross. I finally realized how God saw me—righteous because of what Jesus did at Calvary. Jesus's blood washed me clean. Oh, how I am so grateful to God! I now often share my past wounds. I find by speaking aloud about my past hurts I become free in Christ. I've learned to be bold, courageous, and not to fear, for God is with me.

Can you identify with Vickie? Are you harboring the thought that renewal is for someone else, but not for you? Have you accepted God's invitation, received His Son as your savior, moved through life with Him, but you repeatedly trip on past mistakes? Perhaps you don't believe God wants you free from guilt or shame. Brennan Manning said, "God weeps over us when shame and self-help immobilize us."[5]

God offers more than salvation. He promises an abundant life apart from and above the cares of this world—past, present, and future; yesterday, today, and forever. God calls us to live in a different dimension. Once we meet our true love, we can know our true identity rests in Him. We must let his opinion of us speak louder to us than our past. We must allow the truth of the Word of God to thwart the lies the accuser wants us to believe. John Egan said, "Define yourself as radically loved by God. This is the true self. Every other identity is an illusion."[6]

Many women are wounded. They mourn in silence, yearning for freedom, yet remain unable to acknowledge the love of God. They can't bring themselves to reach out for the hand of God. Disabling circumstances sap their strength, often beyond their control, yet they don't respond to God's invitation to get back up. Why do some choose to live life in a state of numbness? Because they believe renewal is for friends, husband, parents, even children—anyone but them. Some think their damaged emotions are too ruined for God to heal. They don't trust him with their pain. They need to see that the power to get back up begins when the believing starts. That's what trusting God is all about.

There *are* ways to increase your chances of survival in a fall, whether it is accidental, from scaffolding, or recreational, as in the case of a skydive. Together on our journey through *Get Back Up*, we will discover ways to not only survive, but to thrive when God helps us up. These lessons, when applied, can prepare us for the time when life knocks us flat on our faces. We know that it's not *if* but *when* we fall.

The desired result is to victoriously get back up and joyfully walk on in renewed hope. Take the hand of God; allow God to help you work through your heartaches and hard times, and you will be ushered into a place of abundant, complete healing. Joy is the result. Its presence replaces your gloom and despair with warm radiant hope. You have a choice: to stand alone as a prisoner of your pain or move with God in liberty. How will you respond when the future brings fear and anxiety? Remember, you are offered a grace-filled, guilt-free *life* because of Jesus Christ. Each day the choice is yours. Reach out, take His hand, and walk with Him—if you want to soar. He will take off your chains! This kind of truth ignites your faith. It transforms your behavior to reflect your belief about God. The Holy Spirit beckons you to rise up in response to the truth; He invites you to get up and join him in living an abundant life.

....

Study Questions for
Chapter 1: Take My Hand

....

1. Describe the time, date, and location you accepted
    God's invitation. If you haven't accepted his invita-
    tion, take a few minutes to pray this prayer: "Dear
    God, I accept your invitation of love. Thank you for
    giving your son, Jesus, to die in my place. I accept
    the cleansing You offer through the shed blood of
    Jesus Christ. Thank you for forgiving my sins. I
    commit my life to live for You. I want to depend on
    You for everything I need. In Jesus's name, Amen."
    Journal your feelings.

2. Is there an area in your life where you have trouble
    accepting His love?

3. Think about the part of your life where you might
    still be holding onto guilt. Why does God want you
    to be free from that guilt?

4. What choices could you make to enhance your re-
    lationship with the only One who loves you just as
    you are?

5. How can you express your joy to someone else this
    week?

2

Grab onto Truth

Alan Magee, a gunner on a B-17 with the 303rd Bomb Group of the U.S. 8th Air Force, was on a mission to St. Nazaire, France, in January of 1943, when enemy fire set his bomber aflame. He was thrown from the plane before he had a chance to put on his parachute, fell 20,000 feet, and crashed onto the roof of the St. Nazaire train station. His arm was badly injured, but he eventually recovered from that and other injuries. Alan Magee knew how to fall properly and how to land.[1]

Magee survived a long fall because he knew to do three very simple things: bend the knees, relax, and land feet-first. Nothing is more important than bending the knees when landing after a fall. Sounds simple? Research has shown that having one's knees bent on impact significantly reduces the impact force, up to thirty-six-fold. Another way to increase your chances of survival during a long-distance fall is to relax. Relaxing—especially as you near the ground—is easier said than done, although studies of long-fall survivors have shown that those who reported being relaxed suffered, on average, far less severe injuries than those who reported being panicked or tense. Finally, Magee knew to keep his feet and legs tightly together so that both feet hit the ground at the same time. Landing feet-first concentrates the impact force on a small area and allows your feet and legs to absorb the brunt of the impact.

Many spiritual applications are available for free-fall techniques. I've learned these techniques through trial and error, by falling and asking God to help me up again. The first spiritual application parallel to surviving a long fall is landing with both feet together. This is a posture of prayer in an Orthodox service, with feet placed directly under one's hips; standing in the upright position, the participant is fully physically engaged in the liturgy. The feet are the foundation, allowing the mind, body, and soul completeness in worship. The longer I spend standing, I've found I don't notice the emotional and spiritual effort it takes or that the leg and back muscles ache much anymore—my full attention is on my Savior and giving Him glory. The next application is the posture of bent knees in prayer. Kneeling in prayer is a way to show humility and submission to God. Relaxing while in the kneeling position shows God your dependence on Him as you direct your full attention toward hearing Him speak assurance into your life. Standing, kneeling, and relaxing; these are now familiar postures of prayer, sometimes almost reflexive in my personal time with God. But it hasn't always been this way.

New Beginnings

I was a new Christian, enthusiastic about God, which motivated me to graduate from high school. This was a miracle in itself, since I was truant most of my junior year. My passion was the Bible; an unquenchable desire to learn more about God and His word compelled me to earn money to pay my way through Bible college.

I skipped carefree through college and enjoyed newfound independence and friendships. Every experience at this stage of my Christian walk became exhilaration—dorm life, studying, and even the cafeteria food tasted like my mom's homemade apple pie. College life—even in the midst of writing term papers and studying for exams—was better than any chemical high I had ever experienced. It all seemed like a never-ending Christian party celebration.

I needed to complete a course requirement for my senior year, so I changed to a new ministry and met Paul Giesbrecht. We had many interests in common, but what caught my attention was Paul's sense of humor, passionate love for God, and huge heart for ministry. Our romance was better than a fairytale; we were best friends throughout our senior year and served God together in the ministry. Marriage would be our happy ending.

The year after graduation, we worked in different ministries, seeing each other off and on. We were inseparable and in the fall became engaged; our magical wedding was June 27, 1981. Soon after, Ben Giesbrecht, my father-in-law, a sweet and kind man, was diagnosed with kidney cancer. Paul made trips from Orange County, California, north to Bakersfield nearly every weekend the summer of 1982. We weighed the pros and cons with lengthy discussions and much prayer. We decided to move to Bakersfield to be closer to Paul's mom and dad.

Relocating to a new home came in January 1983, from sunny and dry eighty-three-degree weather in Fullerton to a city covered with dense morning fog and penetrating cold. I became depressed, deathly sick, and began to believe I had married the wrong person. I was angry with Paul for deceiving me into marrying him and moving us to Bakersfield. I wanted out.

I had a difficult time believing God had a plan for my life after that. *How could a loving God move me to a cold, dark, ugly place like this?* I hated myself, my life, and my marriage. It was my husband's fault that we were exiled in Bakersfield.

The Difficulty of Nonbelief

Believing God's plan is best is a crisis of the will. I didn't have confidence that God knew what He was doing when He moved Paul and me to Bakersfield. I loved living by the beach, basking in the sun, and the camaraderie of our college friends. The desert certainly was not my idea of an oasis. Things weren't going my way. I had to blame someone, so I took it out on my husband.

Eve was deceived by the serpent into thinking Adam didn't have the facts right. She didn't believe God had the couple's best interests in mind. Eve depended on her inconsistent intuition and allowed rationalization to take her away from the truth until she believed the lie. Her

lot involved a succession of illogical and irrational decisions, which revolved around what she felt and thought
was best. We are deceived when we feel we can't trust God
with our situation and don't believe He can help us. This
is where I found myself. I was in a situation I didn't like,
didn't plan, and wanted to change.

Doubt is the opposite of belief. The only anecdote for
nonbelief is to accept the truth. Those who believe God
can put their faith in Him in any circumstance. Once we
understand God's character, we can trust Him and believe
He loves us. In spite of immobilizing circumstances, we
can choose to move gracefully and freely through trials.

Belief doesn't just happen. It's a conscious choice to
put one's hope in something worthy of trust. It is having
faith in Someone who is reliable. One of God's character
qualities is His faithfulness; He is worthy of our trust. He
is constant, unwavering, dependable, and reliable. Faithfulness is His fiber; it is His being. He will not change.
The condition of mistrusting God is deception because we
have chosen to see God other than how He really is.

"There are areas of deception common to many Christian women including lies about God, sin, priorities, marriage, family, and emotions," Nancy Leigh DeMoss said
in *Lies Women Believe.* "These are at the root of women's
struggles; we must deal honestly with women's delusions
and illusions and focus on the truth of God's Word—the
only thing that leads to true freedom."[2]

The Abyss of Deception

Deception is clever; it tricks us and makes us yearn for what we don't have. The media tells us we must own a certain car, fit into a particular brand or small enough size of clothing, or enjoy the latest fad for contentment. We are bombarded with false advertising enhanced to manipulate us to buy things that we either can't afford or don't need.

Yet, for some of us, the lies that pierced our emotions at a very young age continue to deceive us. These haunt us, affecting our self-talk and influencing our present-day decisions. I was ten years old when comments were made about me in the ballet class locker room. *You are fat; you look like a sausage in a leotard; why do you wear your hair that way?* These poison darts affected my self-perception for over two decades. To tame the lie, I was told to use the phrase, "Sticks and stones may break your bones, but words will never harm you." It didn't work; the lie increased in size and was amplified as I reached adulthood.

Lies never stay the same; over time they always grow into something bigger and more harmful. That's why we must choose God's truth above what we think or what we have been told about ourselves. The lies I heard from other children and believed are now tamed by understanding my identity in Christ. I share them here to offer you insight and direction.

Lie #1: "You are fat," translated into "You are not good enough."
God's truth: "You are worth the life of my Son."

Lie #2: "You are clumsy," translated into "You are
   not worthy."
God's truth: "You get your identity from what I
   (God) have done for you."

Lie #3: "You are boring," translated into "You are
   not popular."
God's truth: "You get your identity from what I
   (God) say about you."

Lie #4: "You can't do anything right," translated
   into "You won't amount to anything."
God's truth: "Your belief in what I (God) am ca-
   pable of determines your behavior."

Belief Brings Relief

Holding close to truth is how you believe God and learn
to take Him at His Word. Essentially, it means to maintain freedom from deception. We must devote ourselves
to search out and find truth. Devoting ourselves to something, according to *Webster's*, "is the choice to be set apart
or dedicated exclusively to."[3] If we dedicate ourselves to
find out solely what God thinks about us, the impact of
the opinions and accusations of others is diminished. On
our own, we cannot undo the lies we have believed since
childhood. God helps us to untangle the knots of deception so we are free to experience truth. "Your attitudes, actions, responses, and reactions of life's circumstances are
greatly affected by what you believe about yourself," Dr.
Neil T. Anderson said.[4] Only truth can untangle the knots

of deception and renew our minds to display God's glory
in the way we live.

The Grip of Grace

God showed me His truth that helped me overcome the
mental lies I believed for decades. I finally trusted and accepted God's passionate love for me. Ever wonder what it's
like to be loved by someone who knows us better than anyone else? God knows your heart better than anyone, so you
can trust Him to take the lead. Ever yearn to be loved unconditionally, with no strings attached? God's love is unconditional and not self-seeking; He doesn't need anything from
you. He only wants your love in return. And this love shows
you where to go. God knew you before you were born, so let
Him lead you. When you choose to believe this, it will make
a difference in every thought you have and everything you
do. You can be confident He is taking you the best way.

I remember when I was young, my daddy and I would
dance to the Glenn Miller Band. In our first attempt to glide
across the living room, I couldn't keep up with his steps and
tripped him. We ended up in a giggling heap on the floor.
"Put your feet on top of mine," Daddy said. I lifted my right
foot and placed it on his left foot and then did the same with
my left on to his right foot. Together, we flitted and twirled
as one, perfectly synchronized. I could stay in step as long
as my feet were planted on my daddy's. His strong arms
held me tight as I stood firmly on his feet. I held on tight to
this truth and grasped the fullness of God's passion for me;
I could confidently stand firm on the supporting foot of
love.

The second part of understanding your identity in Christ is about security. It's difficult to move forward when you feel guilty. Even small steps can be an effort. But you do not have to be victimized by your past, held captive to your thoughts, or imprisoned by how others perceive you. Trusting God moves you ahead unhindered; your progress becomes secure in guilt-free, grace-filled freedom and hope. You are safe. Speaking God's word aloud with authority helps you renew your mind.

You can take control of your thoughts and say aloud, "There is now no condemnation for those who are in Christ Jesus." (Romans 8:1 [NIV]) Applying God's word to your circumstances can move you from deception to truth. Doubt, worry, and fear are just a few deceptions the enemy uses to take your eyes off of Jesus Christ. Instead of listening to the voice of the serpent or relying on your own intuition or feelings, you must tune your ears to recognize God's voice and heed His word. He is your defender. He will protect you; you are sheltered because of His stability. You must believe He can fight your battles. Francis McNutt said, "If the Lord Jesus Christ has washed you in His own blood and forgiven you of all your sins, who are you to refuse to forgive yourself?"[5]

The third part of identity in Christ is that God said you are important. It takes trust to allow someone to help you up after a fall. God values you so highly, you can follow Him without fear through any twist or turn life brings. God has a plan for you, in the good and the bad things that come your way. Letting this truth saturate your thoughts can be a scary process. You must allow Him to change your view from insecurity to confidence. Your part is to recognize God has your best in mind. "Remember God's greatest pleasure is to be believed. His greatest pain is to be doubted."[6]

Missteps

When things go wrong, we often lose our footing; we slip and fall. We question God's love and we wonder, *What have I done to deserve this?* These thoughts frequently plagued my husband and me after our move. He and I were under an enormous amount of stress. Small doses of tension can be productive, but too much of it can produce other problems; we were beginning to experience the fallout of stress. Paul and I worried about finances, which led to sleepless nights, unsolved arguments, and marital frustration.

I felt overwhelmed, emotionless. How about you? Have you ever felt so numb you could not feel God's stabilizing embrace? Did God seem so distant it felt like He dropped you? Did you let go of His hand?

Jean's Story

Jean heard my message in Arizona and shared her story of rediscovering her love for God. She wrote:

Sheryl, I thought I had gone off the deep end. There have been a lot of bumps in the road along the way, from my dad dying in my arms to me trying to get my spiritual life in order. Just when I thought I had it together the pastor left. The last straw was when my husband of seventeen years divorced me. If that wasn't enough, the new pastor left the church for another parish. I finally said, That's it! I don't need God or Jesus. In 1991, I gave up my faith; I quit the church all together. I thought, if God allowed this to happen to me, I don't need or want him. Your talk helped me put my head back on my shoulders; your explanation of God's passionate love helped me realize how to accept God's love and feel his presence in my life. Because of this newfound truth, I can love myself and see that God's love is good. Thank you, your sister in Christ, Jean.

Jean learned to firmly stand on the supporting foot of God's love in just one weekend. She learned how to grasp God's truth for herself. She overcame the lies she'd believed in the past and understood her true identity in Him. Jean's case is not uncommon. Women need to be reminded about God's stabilizing, unconditional love. No matter what happens, God's love *is* our constant support. Christ's finished work on the cross helps women discover they are unconditionally loved, foundationally safe, and unequivocally important; set free to step in tandem with God's purposes.

There is power in speaking aloud the truth of what God thinks about us. You will find statements of truth at the end of this chapter: a list of every person's identity in Christ. Along with each of the three sections are Bible verses and statements taken directly from scripture, itemizing who God said we are. I recommend you read these statements aloud as often as possible to underscore your identity in Christ. When you understand your identity in Christ, you can successfully live the abundant life

He promises. This is how one moves with the rhythm of God's grace. Use these statements regularly to remind yourself of His implicit truth.

Surrender

It took me a while to move from a stiff, reluctant walk to a flowing graceful stroll. The winter of 1983 was a difficult time. Months passed and the fog lifted, literally. The weather grew warmer, and by March I had made a few women friends. We prayed and read Scripture together. We encouraged each other to be faithful, God-believing wives. I began to realize God had a purpose for me to fulfill in Bakersfield, and in the process I fell back in love with my husband. I prayed God would use me however He chose.

Henrietta Mears, founder of Gospel Light, when asked if she could redo any part of her life, said, "Believe God more."[7] Our faith will deepen as we choose to model Mear's wisdom, and our trust will increase. We will move from deception into truth as we fall into God's wise, loving arms, trusting Him with abandon.

Study Questions for
Chapter 2: Grab onto Truth

1. Describe your crisis of belief and explain how belief brings relief.

2. List one introductory truth and a scripture reference.

3. Use the "In Christ I Am" bookmark on the next page to speak aloud the truth of your identity in Christ.

4. Why is negative self-talk detrimental to your identity in Christ?

5. Explain a recent opportunity where you've had to surrender.

In Christ I Am: Bookmark

*"Understanding your identity in Christ
is absolutely essential to your success at living
the victorious Christian life!"*

In Christ
I Am Loved ...
I am forgiven of all my sins.
"Love covers over a multitude of sins" (I Peter 4:8 [NIV]).

I am loved for all eternity.
"I have loved you with an everlasting love. I have drawn you with loving-kindness" (Jeremiah 31:3 [NIV]).

I am surrounded by God's love.
"The Lord's unfailing love surrounds the [wo]man who trusts in Him."(Psalm 32:10 [NIV]).

I can love myself.
"Love your neighbor as yourself" (Leviticus 19:18 [NIV]).

I am able to love others.
"Dear friends, let us love one another for love comes from God" (I John 4:7 [NIV]).

I Am Safe …
I am declared not guilty.
"Therefore, there is now no condemnation for those who are in Christ Jesus … " (Romans 8:1 [NIV]).

I am secure in Christ's love.
"May those who love you be secure" (Psalm 122:6 [NIV]).

I am protected by God.
"Fear of man will prove to be a snare but whoever trusts in the Lord is kept safe" (Proverbs 29:25 [NIV]).

I am not afraid.
"There is no fear in love. But perfect love drives out fear." (I John 4:18 [NIV]).

I am free from Satan's harm.
"We know that anyone born of God does not continue to sin; the one who was born of God keeps him safe, and the evil one cannot harm him" (I John 5:18 [NIV]).

I am defended by God.
"The name of the Lord is a strong tower, the righteous run to it and are safe" (Proverbs 18:10 [NIV]).

I Am Important …

I am God's masterpiece.

"For we are God's masterpiece. He has created us anew in Christ Jesus, so that we can do the good things he planned for us long ago" (Ephesians 2:10 [NLT]).

God has a meaningful purpose for my life.

"For I know the plans I have for you, declares the Lord, plans to prosper you and not to harm you, plans to give you hope and a future" (Jeremiah 29:11 [NIV]).

I am fulfilling God's plan.

"The Lord's purpose prevails" (Proverbs 19:21b [NIV]).

I am part of God's eternal purpose.
" … according to His eternal purpose which he accomplished in Christ Jesus our Lord" (Ephesians 3:11 [NIV]).

I am free to approach God in confidence.
"In him and through faith in him we may approach God with freedom and confidence" (Ephesians 3:12 [NIV]).

God is working in my life to accomplish His will.
" … for it is God who works in you to will and to act according to his good purpose" (Philippians 2:13 [NIV]).

"The more you reinforce who you are in Christ, the more your behavior will reflect your beliefs about God."[8]

3

Let Grudges Go

Nicholas Alkemade was the tail gunner in a British Lancaster bomber on a night mission to Berlin in March of 1944 when German fighters attacked his plane. The captain ordered the crew to bail out; Alkemade looked back into the plane and was shocked to see his parachute in flames. He chose to jump without a parachute rather than to stay in the burning plane. He fell 18,000 feet and landed in trees, underbrush, and snowdrift. He had twisted his knee and sustained a few cuts, but was otherwise all right. Alkemade had known how to fall and how to land in the event of an unsuccessful skydive.[1] He put his skills into action to increase the surface area on which he would land. Skydivers call this the spread eagle. If you position yourself face-down, with your back arched, your arms overhead, palms down and legs back, you will understandably want to slow down before landing. Using the spread-eagle survival method, chances of survival from a long fall are high.

I've thought about how this method applies to me spiritually, and I have taken this approach in my prayer time.

Face-down on the floor, I've tried this spread-eagle form and prayer used by Martin Luther: "Lord, here am I, save me." We should be desperate for a deeper relationship with God. What I love about using the spread-eagle process is that I bring nothing with me to my prayer time—no props, such as devotionals, Bible studies, concordances, Bibles, or even my journal. It's just God and me. I am relying totally on Him and what I've received from Him in the past. Eyes closed, face-down on the floor, I am humbled, prostrate in His presence. When I pour out my heart to Him, I wait on His presence, and He meets me. This spiritual discipline is part of my worship now; it's almost a habit. I found out how to worship when I had to worship.

Flat on My Face

Years later, as a young wife and new mother, I ran with wonder following God in abandon until several harsh jolts of unforeseen circumstances stopped me cold. In my home daycare business, I watched over three eighteen-month-old toddlers, including my son, Ben. One day, these well-fed youngsters began to bite each other. It took months to get them to behave and gnaw on something else.

Weeks later, before the first problem could be solved, our five-year-old daughter Sarah brought us another crisis. She was losing her baby teeth, but her adult teeth were not growing in on schedule. Our pediatric dentist referred us to UCLA Children's Hospital. Countless hours were spent in doctor's offices and laboratories while various tests were given. The procedures were followed by days of appointments with panels of curious pediatricians, X-ray technologists, and bone specialists. They were stumped. When the results came in, Sarah was diagnosed with a rare bone disease: hypophosphatasia type four. Though all were unsure of treatment options, we were told she would probably outgrow it in time.

Paul and I were still reeling over that bit of news when we received a phone call that forever changed our lives. We were about to visit the senior pastor's house for fellowship and dessert when the telephone rang. The pastor said, "Paul, don't bother coming over tonight, I'd like you to turn in your job resignation." For no biblical or ethical reason, my husband was fired from his pastoral position. We found ourselves in a divorce—not from each other, but from the church.

We physically left the fellowship of the congregation and church staff, and although we didn't move out of town, we parted ways with friends, youth group families, and partners in ministry. There was an emotional ripping and tearing as we separated ourselves from those we had grown to love. Not only did my husband lose a job, we lost our church family. I became the sole financial supporter of our little family of four, with only my part-time daycare job. Feeling like I carried the weight of the world, I worried how we might pay our mortgage, the stack of medical bills, and several bad business loans. Suddenly, a few biting babies didn't seem like such a big problem.

Depressed and in despair, it felt like all my hopes and dreams had died; my fairytale life would never have a happy ending. Much like Lot's wife, I was frozen in anger, a statue of bitterness. I wondered, *How could this hap-*

pen in a church? Why was my husband fired? I vowed, *I will never forgive the people who hurt me and my family.*

The Choice to Forgive

All of us will have opportunities to forgive, but some of us will have *many* opportunities. God gave us a way to keep the lines of communication open between Him and us. "We must forgive, so that no advantage is taken of us by Satan, for we are not ignorant of his schemes," the Apostle Paul told us in 2 Corinthians 2:10, 11 (NIV). Forgiveness is a choice; it's a decision, a crisis of the will. Jesus reminds us in Luke 6:36, "Be merciful, just as your Heavenly Father is merciful" (NIV). Although it is still our choice, if we want mercy, we are commanded to be merciful through forgiveness.

It's up to us to remember that our Heavenly Father has granted us *substitutionary forgiveness* through His Son, Jesus. The Old Testament records God's requirement for the blood of a lamb to satisfy the substitutionary requirement. Hebrews 9:22 explains the concept of an innocent life in payment for the sin of a human being; "The law says that almost everything must be made clean by blood, and sins cannot be forgiven without blood to show death" (NCV).

The Lord Jesus is our substitute, literally becoming sin for us. "Look, the Lamb of God, who takes away the sin of the world" (John 1:29 [NIV]). Jesus's crucifixion wounds belonged to us; He was punished in our place to satisfy God's requirement. His sacrifice provided for our righteousness. "Christ had no sin, but God made him become sin so that in Christ we could become right with God"

(2 Corinthians 5:21 [NCV]). The choice to forgive others means no one really forgives without bearing the consequences of the other person's sin. The act of forgiveness is application of the substitution Christ offered to his Heavenly Father for us.

The Grip of a Grudge

We think we are in control when we hold onto grudges and keep track of wrongs against us. We feel we have a right to be angry or keep our distance from someone who has been inappropriate to us. Offenses may seem harmless, but even gossip or misunderstandings can deeply wound us.

Offenses such as robbery, divorce, molestation, and rape can cause us to feel justified to hold onto our pain. We are angry at the events and want revenge on our perpetrators. Karen Scalf Linamen said, "A grudge usually has a legitimate beginning, someone we trust—an acquaintance, friend, or family member—does something that causes us to feel hurt. But here's where that logic goes awry. Too often, we conclude: If I have a right to feel hurt, then I must have a right to feel hurt for a very, very long time."[2]

Identity Crisis

I have a friend who had been in and out of counseling for over twenty years; she'd been on antidepressants and tried various desperate methods to put distance between her and the event that robbed her of childhood innocence. She constantly dredged up the situation; when she'd call or come into a meeting, I would think of the traumatic situation even before she mentioned it. My sweet friend was hooked to the event and to the person who took advantage of her. The event, which lasted only an instant, became her identity. It took her a long time; when she finally did forgive her offender, she allowed God to restore her identity, and it changed her life.

Months later, when Paul and I were still smarting from his expulsion, we noticed we'd become tense and angry whenever we discussed the situation. Remembering the way things were handled or mishandled by the church board, we didn't agree with how his dismissal had played out and even considered a libel suit. Soon we found out the entire episode was planned to secure a place on the staff for the senior pastor's good friend. We'd already questioned the ethics and integrity of the leadership and now we questioned its honesty. And this was a *church* staff?

I transported our daughter to and from the church's preschool program twice each school day, which made matters much worse. We were finally past the fright of her illness, and it was a joy for me to be with her, but I greatly disliked being near the church that had caused us so much pain. I was a stone's throw from the pastor's office, not once, but twice a day, five days a week. It was all I could do not to drive to the other side of the parking lot, barge into the pastor's office, and tell him off. Each day I hoped I might run into him, accidentally—with my car.

Days and months passed while we continued to nurture our hurt and our hate; we were extremely angry and increasingly bitter. My husband and I knew we needed to do something to get over our grudge; we just weren't ex-

actly sure what. We grew more irritable and increasingly
annoyed with each other and the Church. We had forgotten how to dance. Although we didn't know it at the time,
God's plan to rescue us was coming—and in his own perfect timing.

Holding onto grudges is self-deception. We believe we
can control situations by refusing to let go. This doesn't
damage the person we are "begrudging" as much as it
damages us. Max Lucado said, "Grudges are the cocaine of
anger, they require more and more hate to keep it alive."[3]
Resentments are like a cancer. They multiply and intrude
on our mental health, relationships, and sound sleep. That
kind of holding on can become an addiction.

It's Good for Us

Letting go of a grudge is good for your health. Grudges increase tension and stress, deplete energy, cause isolation, and prevent old wounds from healing. Grudges steal
joy, disrupt sleep, and harden hearts and arteries. Such
bitter emotions can even get in the way of prayers. Resentment keeps us in chains unless we recognize it as bitterness. Give up the grudge and our right to get even, and we
will gain peace, sound mind, and a restful sleep.

We can train our minds to refuse to keep score of the
wrongs others have committed against us through the
power of God's word. Remember that 1 Corinthians 13:5
says, "Love keeps no record of wrongs" (NIV). We must
not keep lists of anything that has hurt, angered, offended,
or wronged us. It's only through God's power this is possible. Evagrius Ponticus said, "Resentment casts a cloud

over your prayers ... if you collect injuries and resentments and think you can still pray, you would probably
put water in a bucket full of holes!"[4]

We give God permission to do whatever He wants
with us when we choose forgiveness instead of bitterness.
This is one of the most difficult steps of faith we will ever
take. Martin Luther King, Jr. said, "Forgiveness is not an
occasional act, it is a permanent attitude."[5] Forgiveness
should actually begin at the time of the offense. Forgiveness is the only way to follow God in faith.

June's Story

June from Oklahoma overcame her struggle with unforgiveness. I was the keynote speaker at her church's
women's retreat. She pulled me aside to tell me of her own
success story after my message on forgiveness:

*I worked in an office with many non-Christians. I
wanted to be a witness to my coworkers. My supervisor,
Andy, was demeaning and disrespectful; he spoke cutting comments and harsh words to everyone—and especially to me. Though the circumstances were unbear-
able, I chose to forgive him the minute he offended me,
which was on a regular basis. In fact, each day as I came
to work, my bright and cheery, "Good morning, Andy!"
would be snubbed as he wrinkled up his nose and turned
away. I was determined to show God's love and offer
forgiveness to my offender. An understanding husband
allowed me to vent my frustrations each evening as my
boss only became harsher and meaner, not only to me*

but also to the other employees. The day Andy was fired I had a glimpse of hope. But the next day, I was assigned to help him find a new job. He would come to the office every day; I would retype his résumé and set up job interviews for him. Now even more than before, I was the object of Andy's wrath. For two months, I continued to smile, talk kindly, and greet him with my usual, "Good morning, Andy," yet his anger continued to burn. My professional attitude and helpfulness paid off. One day he got a job. The next day, he was gone from my life. Two weeks later, I received a phone call. It was Andy. "June, I am sorry. It was wrong of me to be so mean to you. Will you forgive me?" I quickly agreed. The fruit of forgiveness is so sweet.

Obviously June found it hard to forgive, but she kept on, and God rewarded her. Truly June's example is commendable; she experienced freedom to forgive and loved her boss, even though he was anything but loveable.

Letting Go

It helps to take these four steps toward getting rid of the grudge.

Step 1: Confess it

We must agree with God about our sin. Blunt honesty can be difficult. It takes a little time to sort out injured feelings. It is essential before we can be healed of an unforgiving spirit. Consider Romans 2:4: "Or do you think lightly of the riches of his kingdom and forbearance and patience, not knowing that the kindness of God leads you to repentance?" (NIV). We show God how we respond to His loving kindness through a sincere desire to get rid of the grudge. The result: in good conscience we admit our sin and humbly repent.

Step 2: Let go of it

We must release our hurt and hate to God. This means giving up our control of the situation and its outcome to Him. We choose to release the offending person when we give him over to our Heavenly Father. Letting go of the grudge means we are choosing not to hold a person accountable for the debt we feel he owes.

Step 3: Name it

Dr. Neil T. Anderson said, "Unless forgiveness visits the core of your emotions, it is incomplete."[6] God has wired us with a need to constantly get rid of pent-up hurt and hate. This purging of the soul restores our right relationship with Him; it's good for us spiritually, physically, and emotionally. We allow Him to do a deep work in us when we name the emotion, identify our feelings, and privately turn them over to God.

Someone at work, for instance, has made a sarcastic, hurtful comment. You feel hostile, bitter, and resentful. Those are attitudes God wants our permission to change in us. He can change us by exposing our weaknesses; if we are sensitive to Him and cooperate with His will, He can use times of struggle for His glory. He can make us better instead of bitter.

I recommend using a simple prayer I learned from

Dr. Neil T. Anderson to help you understand and experience how forgiveness can visit the core of your emotions. It goes like this: "Dear God, I forgive (fill in the person's name)_____for making me feel (describe how you felt at the time of the offense. List every emotion, allowing God to mentally take you back to the time it happened) _____."[7]

Ask God to help you forgive every painful memory and every person associated with it. And then close with this prayer: "Lord, I release all these people into Your hands. I relinquish my right to seek revenge. I choose not to hold on to the hurt and the hate. I let go of my anger and bitterness. Please heal my damaged emotions. In Jesus's name, Amen."

Step 4: Believe it

We give ourselves a gift when we receive God's forgiveness. Have you ever asked God to forgive you, and He's said, "No, sorry, you've run out of forgiveness coupons for today." Absolutely NOT! Jesus was asked, "How many times shall I forgive my brother when he sins against me? Up to seven times?" Jesus answered, "I tell you, not seven times, but seventy-seven times." (Matthew 18: 21–22 [NIV]). God will always forgive us, and, in the same way, we must forgive others.

Set the Captive Free

The best part about forgiveness is that we don't have to do it alone. God asks us to forgive, but He also gives us the ability to do it. Consider Matthew 18:33: "Should you not also have had mercy on your fellow slave, even as I had mercy on you?" (NIV). Remember: Forgiveness is giving ourselves a gift, not giving a gift to the person we've forgiven. In fact, the person we forgive may not ever know we've forgiven him, but God will.

Forgiveness is between God and us. Confessing our forgiveness to someone who has not first asked for it can cause more problems than it solves. Forgiving others should actually begin at the time we are offended, but it can still be accomplished even if the hurt occurred years ago—even if the offender is now deceased.

We should always be willing to forgive if we are asked. This lets the person know we hold nothing against him and fulfills an additional scriptural challenge. Consider the parable of the unforgiving debtor in Matthew 18:21–35. The king offered grace and didn't require the nobleman to repay the financial debt he owed, yet when the nobleman's own employee asked for a grace period, the nobleman threw him in jail. As a consequence of his unforgiveness, the nobleman was thrown in jail. God requires us to forgive others when we are asked, just as He forgives us when we ask Him for forgiveness.

The Rescue

Our daughter continued at her old school about a year after the "divorce." A friend provided her transportation, so I no longer had to keep up with that. We further distanced ourselves from those painful circumstances by settling into our new church. I still felt challenged with this very concept of forgiveness. Our new church was hosting a conference where the idea of giving up the grudge was presented. There were testimonies of the power of finding freedom through forgiveness, as well as biblical teaching on its principles and how to apply them. Homework was assigned to implement those principles. It was recommended we each make a list of people we needed to forgive. I shuddered at the thought, but knew it was time.

The names flew from my pen onto the paper when I first sat down to make my list. The obvious came easily, but the more difficult ones I didn't want to release. I decided I wanted to be completely honest with God after considerable struggle. The list spanned nearly twenty-five years, encompassing seventy-five people. It took God and me an excruciating two hours to pray through them. Allowing forgiveness to visit the core of my emotions proved liberating. Formerly, I was a statue frozen in bitterness. Now I was restored to walk in the freedom of forgiveness.

I went through that list, and I forgave the people who had fired my husband and taken the joy of life away from our family. I took the offenders off my hook and put them on God's. I knew God wanted me to grant them forgiveness, although I didn't think they deserved it. His forgiveness preceded mine; now it was my turn. I allowed God to have His way in the situation, although I might not ever see it resolved here on earth. I forgave them and was now free to move on with my life.

The Results

Six months later, I was meeting a client downtown and happened to run into the president of the elder board of our old church. Our eyes met, locked, and we exchanged greetings. Prior to forgiving all those people, I would have attempted to avoid him altogether, even ducking out a back door. We talked for a few minutes. He wondered how everything was going. I told him we were doing okay. He asked specific questions about the severance package, communication with the board after we left, and how we had been treated by the church and board members. I was shamelessly honest; people were not following through. He initiated another meeting with Paul and the senior pastor. Three things were clear to Paul and me: we desired but had not sought out reconciliation, we knew there were lessons to be learned on all sides, and God was up to something.

A few weeks later, Paul and I met with the board president and the senior pastor at a coffee shop. My heart was totally healed of hurt, anger, and bitterness because I had worked through my unforgiveness. Paul had done the same thing and was glad for the meeting. I finally knew in my own heart that God's mercy, grace, and love are enough to cover any sin committed against us. Paul and I chose to walk in the truth of Ephesians 4:31, 32: "Let all bitterness and wrath and anger and clamor and slander be put away from you with all malice, and be kind to one another, tenderhearted, forgiving each other, just as God in Christ has forgiven you" (NIV).

The meeting began as an exploration of evidence and ended up being a time of healing. It was a God-ordained time. The board president and senior pastor asked whether or not there had been contact with certain people who had promised to follow through with encouraging us.

There had been no contact. They were shocked to find that people had shirked their responsibilities. The senior pastor compassionately apologized for the awkward handling of Paul's dismissal. Both the senior pastor and board president understood our pain and suffering to the point of tears. We had not expected their tears or apology. We accepted both. The four of us joined hands in a time of prayer and praise, glad for restored fellowship. Paul and I hadn't anticipated we would have the opportunity to explain our side of the situation. Thankful, we understood how it felt to be reconciled with fellow brothers in Christ through the power of forgiveness.

God wants you to offer compassion, understanding, and forgiveness to all who offend you. And when an opportunity to explain your side is given to you, with God's strength, accept it and give Him glory. God wants to release you from your frozen state of bitterness to a graceful walk in the freedom of forgiveness.

Study Questions for
Chapter 3: Let Grudges Go

1. Where in scripture do we find the command to forgive?

2. Explain the concept of "substitutionary forgiveness." Use references.

3. What are some of the health problems we can expect if we don't give up a grudge?

4. List the four steps to let go of a grudge.

5. Who is forgiveness between? List references.

6. Make a list of people you need to forgive. Write their names, dates they offended you, and where it happened. Use the prayer in step 3 within the chapter. Take time alone to read the prayer with the person's name out loud, as you itemize the date and location. Commit them to God and relinquish your right to seek revenge.

4

Hanging by a Thread

Vesna Vulovic was a twenty-two-year-old flight atten-
dant on Yugoslav Airlines DC-9 en route from Stockholm
to Belgrade. Unbeknownst to the crew, a bomb had been
planted in the front baggage compartment. The aircraft
was at 33,330 feet, about halfway through the flight, when
the bomb exploded. Vulovic was in the tail section that fell
to the earth, landing at just the right angle on a slope of
snow-covered mountains.

Vulovic was in the right place at the right time. She
had just completed the snack and beverage service and
cleaning up the kitchen area of the cabin. Her attention to
detail and thorough follow-through with a routine activity saved her life. She was inside the tail section, and, like a
protective cover, it helped break her fall. It took seventeen
months to recover from her extensive injuries. Ultimately,
Vulovic was the only survivor of the twenty-eight passengers and crew. In fact, according to the *Guinness Book of
World Records*,[1] she holds the world record for surviving
the highest fall without a parachute. Vulovic's determina-

tion and choices enabled her to be found and rescued. It was as if God saw her hanging by a thread.

As the months sped by, my bitterness left behind, I stepped lightly with the freedom of forgiveness. Yet the rhythm of my life still seemed a little off. I wondered if we'd ever be in ministry in a church again, and I decided it was okay if we weren't.

Paul and I were hired for public-service jobs within months of leaving the pastorate. They seemed like the next best thing to ministry. Paul's job at the local prison was an opportunity to instill hope into the lives of convicts while teaching them job skills. I networked resource services as a social worker with the state of California for parents of children with developmental disabilities. Our professions were rewarding but stressful. We were spread thin by job demands, raising our young family, and volunteering for our new church.

Our young children had multiple health needs. Our toddler son, Ben, was diagnosed with asthma, and anytime he caught a cold, it would develop into bronchitis. Five-year-old Sarah's chronic ear infections since age six months translated into many sleepless nights for all four of us.

The stress of that time came to a head on a cold, weekday winter morning. I had been up late the night before because Paul and I had been fighting about money—again. It was 5:00 a.m.; I'd been up and down every two hours all night, nebulizing Ben's fits of coughing with breathing treatments. When Ben finally fell back to sleep, I laid him down in his crib and wished I could have curled up next to him. It was time for me to decide if he would be well enough to go to daycare or if I should stay home from work.

It didn't take long to conclude that Ben was too sick to go to daycare. Pam, our daycare provider, refused to give nebulizer treatments, so that meant even if Ben could go, I would have to pack everything up and go to the daycare center every two hours to administer the treatments myself. I had used up all my sick time. We couldn't afford time off work without pay, plus I had several important meetings that could not be rearranged. Although it went against my grain as a mother to not be the one to care for my sick baby, I didn't have a choice.

I called Michelle, our college-student babysitter, for her to care for Ben at the house for the day. *It's only one day*, I rationalized as guilt and fatigue took over. I was totally exhausted, racked with worry, and mind numb. I sat at the kitchen table and robotically wrote a list of the day's instructions for the sitter. Remembering the fight from the night before, I wondered why everything in every area of my life was falling apart.

Reality Check

Michelle arrived. I hurried Sarah to the car, hoping to get her to school on time. My heart sank as I dropped her off. Leaving Sarah on the inner-city public school campus where fights were known to occur seemed like another defeat. I longed to home school, but we couldn't afford it. My world would feel so much better if only I could stay home and care for my precious children myself.

During the ten-minute drive to my office in the sanctuary of my car, I let the tears flow freely. As I breathed prayers of desperation, I pulled off the roadway to let the music from the radio calm me down. When the music stopped, a woman's soothing voice expressed how prayer met her needs. She explained how she prayed for her children while they were away from her. An announcer introduced *Focus on the Family*'s daily broadcast as "Mom's In Touch," mothers who gathered in small groups to pray for their children in school. Soon I found out the woman was founder Fern Nichols. She said, "Prayer helped me learn to trust God to protect my children while in public school."[2] I wondered if I could learn to pray like that. Of course prayer was part of my life but not enough to give me hope about specific situations.

Prayer Lesson

After a bit of research, I found a Mom's in Touch (MIT) group. In fact, the MIT leader for Sarah's school was the area coordinator for our county. A few weeks later, at my first meeting, I was a little skeptical, thinking it would probably end up like every other prayer group I'd been in, where my needs had not been met. Too much time wasted talking or problems would come up during prayer meeting. Some women were "prayer hogs," taking up large chunks of time. Others were "prayer snobs" — after a woman had opened her heart and emotions, sharing a struggle, they would take it upon themselves to lecture her during the time of prayer. I entered the room, expecting another big disappointment.

When our leader, Sue, explained the format, I was

intrigued with the simplicity of Mom's in Touch, which utilized four steps: praise, confession, thanksgiving, and intercession. I learned that the foundation of MIT was "praying in one accord." She explained that the first component of our prayer time would focus on praise. The core of Mom's in Touch is simple: talking to God about our children.

The goal of the group was to concentrate on one subject at a time, to hear the heartfelt thoughts of others, and to truly be burden-bearers. This method made MIT more spiritually enriching to me than any other prayer group I had ever been in.

Praise

As our first prayer time began, Sue described how praying scripture during the praise time helps us to pray God's words back to Him. She said we would focus on one of God's character qualities, and this week it was love. I was thrilled to discover there is power in declaring, proclaiming, and confessing who God is and what He does. Sue elaborated that praising God is for our good; it brings freedom and hope. It was encouraging to focus on praising God and enlightening to focus on God and not the situation. As we continued to pray, we looked up more scripture and praised God together.

As Carol read Psalm 136:1–4 aloud, an amazing thing happened: my spirit found many things for which to praise God. While listening to Carol praise God through reading scripture, I worshiped Him, too. I began to worship Him for His love for me. I worshiped Him for His wisdom. I worshiped Him for this time of praise with the prayer group.

When it was my turn to read scripture aloud, I read:

"Who shall separate us from the love of Christ? *Shall trouble or hardship* or persecution or famine or nakedness or danger or sword? ... No in all these things we are more than conquerors through him who loved us" (Romans 8:35–37 [NIV]).

Those words *shall trouble or hardship* began to sink in as I considered my own circumstances.

In the past, my praise time had been more about me than God. It was almost like praising God buttered Him up so I could put my requests before Him. This time it was different. Using scripture helped maintain my focus. I was praising God for His love and nothing else. I was just worshiping Him for loving me. Before, I wanted everything to be fixed. I wanted things to change for my benefit. I wanted my situation to be changed. Suddenly, the Holy Spirit spoke to my heart, proclaiming, "Let Me change you."

Confession

From praise we moved to confession. For several minutes we silently confessed our sins to God. In my own heart I remembered a verse I'd known for years but had never really understood: "If we confess our sins, he is faithful and just to forgive us our sins and to cleanse us from all unrighteousness" (I John 1:9 [NIV]).

I had some major confessing to do. First, I asked God to forgive my self-sufficiency. He showed me I needed not only His help to manage the care of my children, but

I needed to ask for the help of family members. Next, I asked God to forgive my rebellious heart. I confessed my pursuit of interests that drew me away from family time. Then I asked God to forgive my jealous, covetous eyes. I desired other women's lifestyles, homes, jobs, families, and even husbands. I wanted to escape my life. As I went through these areas one by one, God totally purified and healed each of them. I willingly submitted my life to God again and felt totally renewed. I might not have earned a place in the *Guinness Book of World Records* for surviving a plane crash without a parachute, but I learned a spiritual lesson I'd remember and apply for a very long time.

Thanksgiving

Once we completed the time of confession, we moved into thanksgiving. We collectively took turns thanking God for answering our prayers from the week before. When it was my turn, I thanked God for helping me find my way to this prayer group. The other moms chimed in:

"Dear God, you are so good. We have prayed for new moms to come to our group, and you have answered."

"Heavenly Father, thank you for bringing Sheryl to us. She is such a blessing."

I thought, *Could it be I am an answer to prayer?* Immediately, I knew this prayer group was God's answer to *my* prayers, too.

Intercession

The fourth and last step in the MIT format is intercession. Intercession or praying on behalf of someone else is
one of our highest callings. The apostle Paul tells us, "because he (Jesus) always lives to intercede for them" (Hebrews 7:25b [NIV]). Jesus is seated at the right hand of God,
always praying for us. When we pray scriptural prayers
over our children, we release the power of God.

We were each assigned a portion of scripture to read
over our children and shown how to pray the scriptural
prayer over their lives. At the start of the prayer time, I'd
wondered about my needs being met. Now, as I prayed for
other people's children, I got it—prayer was a sacrificial gift
we could give to each other, our children, and also to God.

It was then my turn to share my request for intercession.
I wanted to vent my frustration so I could gain the sympa-
thy I thought I deserved. Instead, I chose to follow the MIT
format. I read aloud: "It was good for me to be afflicted so
that I might learn your decrees" (Psalm 119:71 [NIV]).

And then I prayed that God would give me compassion
toward Ben and Sarah and help me to love sacrificially. In
turn, each of the other women prayed for my family members as well. As the moms prayed, I felt immediate release.
The peace of God lifted my tired, burdened heart, and the
heaviness was replaced with a little bit of joy and a lot of
hope.

God's Groupie

I met Elora from Portland, Oregon, one of the organizers for a women's retreat. I was the keynote speaker. She was going through a huge personal transition; it might have been easier for her to pull away from the group and not be involved in the retreat planning. God was moving her out of her comfort zone. Her husband was being transferred two-thousand miles away from everything they knew. God was asking them to trust Him with a new group. After one of my presentations, Elora said, "The phrase *I am safe* resonated with me. In two weeks, I am moving far across the country to Pennsylvania. I will leave everything I know—a home, the familiar, kids' schools, and our church. I am learning what it means to live like I am safe in God's hands." Elora chose to trust the safety of her relationship with God, first. As she stepped into the unknown, she knew God would provide the groups she and her family needed: a Bible teaching church, fellowship, accountability, and service opportunities.

Elora's choice to trust God with her needs for a group and mine were similar. I'd tried to bring prayer groups together countless times before, but this time was different. God put the group together by bringing me to MIT. He also picked the prayer method he wanted me to learn. In the past, I had picked who would be in the group and what material we would use to pray or study. This time I took a risk: I chose to be vulnerable with the women in the group. I ventured out of my comfort zone, trusting God with the group and the method. In the process, I not only found new friends and prayer partners, but I also found hope.

The book of Jude was given to encourage the church to be faithful, to bind together to function as a healthy group. This kind of body life doesn't just happen, it must be a concerted effort to get together and do life in the format of small groups. Jude 20–21 (NIV) sums it up well, "But you, dear friends build yourselves up in your most holy faith and pray in the Holy Spirit. Keep yourselves in God's love as you wait for the mercy of our Lord Jesus Christ to bring you to eternal life." As we mature in Christ, we must allow God to direct us to include people in our lives and be open to learning new methods we might not have chosen. With MIT, the common thread that brought us moms together was praying for our children. Through the desire to pray for our children at their schools, we experienced God's character while learning how to love our children and each other in a sacrificial way.

I felt a renewed sense of hope driving home that afternoon from the MIT prayer time. Instead of despair, I anticipated solutions to my problems. A confident assurance washed over me that, during times of need or plenty, God would provide answers. My faith became revived. No longer would I find myself hanging on by a thread.

Study Questions for
Chapter 4: Hanging by a Thread

1.   Describe the author's reality check. Explain what she did next.

2.   Give details about a recent situation where you've received a reality check.

3.   List the Mom's In Touch four steps to prayer.

4.   How is the MIT method different than what you have been doing?

5.   How is the method similar?

6.   How does a prayer group help us function as the body of Christ?

5

Alone and Afraid

Christmas Eve 1971. Juliane Koepcke awoke on the Amazon jungle floor strapped into her airplane seat, surrounded by fallen holiday gifts. Her LANSA Flight 508 from Lima to Pucallpa, Peru, had crashed during a thunderstorm. Six crewmembers and eighty-six passengers had been on board. Everyone else, including her mother, had perished in the crash. She had fallen two miles down and remarkably had survived. Injured and alone, she remembered her mother's last words: "I love you." Mindful of her mother's words and biologist father's practical advice, "To find civilization in the jungle, follow water," for nine days, Koepcke ate hard candy, drank dirty water, and made her way through the dense vegetation; wading from tiny streams to larger ones, passing crocodiles, and poking mud with a stick to scare away stingrays. On the tenth day, Juliane saw a canoe tethered to the shoreline. She climbed up to an embankment where lumberjacks found her. Kopcke had survived by using common sense, love, and faith.[1]

I've waded through and found my way beyond a jungle of my own making, and when I implemented a discipline of prayer, it made me thirsty for more. I worked hard to strengthen it by praying scripture. Each evening I'd set the coffeemaker on automatic so it would brew by the time I got up. I'd plan ahead by setting out my Bible, devotional, and prayer notebook, ready for my morning time with God. My early morning "meeting with the King of kings" was the only way I could begin my day, even if it meant getting up at least thirty minutes before the other family members and losing sleep. Some days I would literally stumble into God's presence, but it didn't matter: I was determined to keep my commitment to Him.

"It's better to be sleep deprived than God deprived," said Jill Briscoe. I found this to be true as I experienced answers to prayer. I endeavored to be consistent in my study of the names of God and by praying scriptural prayers. It was amazing how much better I managed my schedule and saw breakthroughs in important relationships with my husband, children, and job as a social worker. Paul found gratification as he taught trade skills to inmates at the prison. It was good to be behind the scenes, low-key, and anonymous at our new church instead of the fishbowl pastor's life we had experienced before.

My life was full, and so was my heart. I worked in my full-time job as a social worker, along with joyfully managing my home; I discovered a new respect for my husband and a fresh love for my children. A real serendipity was that I found many opportunities for ministry in my job. I became more secure in my skills as a mother and understood the emotional needs of our family. God's continued provision for me and my family was evident.

Paul and I considered joining our new church and decided to take the new members' class. One Sunday morning, the senior pastor pulled us aside and said, "I don't know what happened at your other church or why you are here, but take as long as you need to heal." The senior pastor's words were just what we needed. The new church was the perfect place for us to continue to recover from the bumps and bruises from the other ministry. We were glad we weren't expected to serve immediately because we welcomed time off to heal from our previous church experience.

A year or so passed. We settled in and saw needs in the church we were eager to meet. I volunteered in our children's Sunday school classes, and Paul took on a teaching role in an adult Sunday school class. After about six months, he was offered a paid pastoral position working with divorced or never-been-married single adults and college students on staff at our new church. We wondered if it might be time for us to get back into church ministry.

Beginning at the End

Paul was a positive force and role model for the inmates, which made it a difficult decision for him to leave his job at the prison. He'd never worked with singles before, so we decided to find out more about the population of divorced and widowed adults. We read about how the Church, just like the world, is affected by the ravages of divorce. A recent statistic quotes: "Marriages formed today have about a 41 to 43 percent chance of ending in divorce."[2] Paul quickly realized he'd be working with a different type of prisoner—those held captive in a prison of their past. He was up for the challenge and excited about the new opportunity and even more thrilled about the reconnection with the Church.

There was a little damage control needed for the programs Paul took over. They had not had a consistent, loving leader in years. Amazingly, our painful encounters from the past helped us to relate to some of the issues the new divorcees felt. Our divorce from our last church had many parallels to what happens when a marriage comes apart. We shared with the singles the principles we learned about healing relationships. The extreme hurt of leaving our last ministry became a tangible object lesson, which helped us understand and take on some of the burdens of the brokenhearted—and it was well received. Many who had experienced catastrophic loss because of separation, divorce, or death now found how to gain freedom through forgiveness and a healthy mindset to move on with life.

Divorce's Dilemma

We could help singles work through their thoughts of bitterness, but like an angry evil twin, they spoke out against their exes when sharing overwhelming feelings of abandonment. Most had been dumped by their spouse. They felt like castaways. "Abandon," defined by Webster's, means "to give up."[3] Abandonment is best described by these verbs: deserted, left behind, rejected, and neglected.

Abandonment issues in the marriage casualties that came into the singles' group amplified the reality of today's family fragmentation. As there are families pulled apart in every direction by divorce and custody battles, abandonment is a huge issue. Every day spouses and children are left behind. To avoid paying child support or alimony, the one leaving might keep his whereabouts a secret and/or fail to support the family. The sense of being unwanted or rejected has a significant impact on a person's self-perception but also affects how that person stays in touch with her feelings and desires. Abandonment can breed codependence, which, as defined by John Bradshaw, "is a disease characterized by a loss of identity. To be codependent is to be out of touch with one's feelings and desires."[4]

Once a spouse is rejected by another, she is often drawn to the exact same personality type. Let's say a divorced woman was married to an alcoholic or drug addict, and she hoped to help him through his problems. Ultimately she becomes an enabler, and, instead of actually helping the spouse quit, she contributes to the problem, sometimes in unhealthy ways. We watched divorced women in our group fall into destructive and self-abasing situations with men in the group.

"Abandonment issues are difficult to successfully heal and resolve; they are just so deeply seated and intense," said Steve Cooper in his article, "The Legacy of Father's Loss." He continued, "You have abandonment issues if you become enraged if your boyfriend is late for a date, you become possessive or jealous of your significant other's time, obsessing about the possibility that your beloved will cheat on you. If you show me a couple where one member has abandonment issues, I'll show you a couple that fights frequently, loudly, perhaps even violently. The classic story for someone, male or female, who is abandoned by their parent in their childhood is that they deliberately but unconsciously select a spouse whose very nature is to cut off, betray and abandon by having an affair. God wants to heal our unresolved childhood wounds and our very natures to be free of reenacting our childhood issues with our selected partners just filling in for our parents. The saddest cases are when they recover from horrible rejections and select a new spouse who turns around and cheats on them as well. I tell my clients that it is bad enough that we had to end our childhoods, but the kicker is that if we get involved in a relationship as an adult, we will inevitably have to experience that very same pain over again."[5]

Many women stay in their marriages much longer than they care to admit because they fear being alone. Most of them also struggle with feelings of depression. When I asked them how they were doing, they said they weren't interested in any of their usual hobbies. They admitted they felt unworthy and, along with this unhealthy self-image, had problems with sleeping, no appetite, overeating, low energy, and lack of concentration. I knew these were signs of depression. I began sharing the *In Christ I Am* list with them. Once they began to believe what God thinks about them and decided it mattered more than the opinion of anyone else, they developed stronger boundaries, and their damaged emotions began to heal. Though I was struggling in my marriage and life, I looked around at the women in the group and realized I was much better off than them.

Nobody's Home

For a while, I successfully juggled many hats. But the stress of working, mothering, being a pastor's wife and ministry leader cost me my morning quiet time with God. I thought, *I don't know anyone at the church.* My life was full, yet my identity was empty; I didn't feel like I knew myself anymore. I wasn't sure what to make of it. I buried my feelings of insecurity, isolation, and aloneness in a busy schedule and purposefully kept an overflowing calendar.

I was worn out, stressed out, felt abandoned as a servant of God—even though I had two beautiful children, a lovely home, and a steady income. I had a husband, something most of the women in the singles' group were jealous of—yet I felt as if I was losing my mind. Every Sunday, I would go to church and hang out with the college kids or the single adults, yet I felt like I had no close friends at church. Although I was very involved with the ministries, with people around all the time, something was missing: I was sure God didn't love me anymore. Thinking that more things to do would help me better organize what I already committed to, I took on even more volunteer jobs at the church. This not only brought more strain on the family and tension in my job, it also caused me to become depressed. Most nights, I barely slept through the night, and most mornings I struggled to get myself out of bed.

I would welcome a "mental-health day" when one of our kids was sick. One time in our pediatrician's office waiting room, I flipped through a *Parent's* magazine. I glanced at an article: "Personal Stress Solutions: In a recent

Roper Starch Worldwide survey of 30,000 people between the ages of 30 to 65 in thirty countries showed women who work full-time and have children under the age of thirteen reported the greatest stress worldwide. Nearly one in four mothers who work full-time and have children under thirteen feel stress almost every day."[6]

I knew my stress level was linked to my mental health: I was depressed and discouraged. I saw myself in the article—I felt stress every day, and I was sure I felt the greatest stress in the world.

Hagar's Story

We studied one of the names of God for each session in our weekly MIT prayer time. One week, we read Genesis 16, the account of barren Sarai's maid, Hagar, chosen to bear Abraham's child. Now pregnant by Abraham, she was abused by her jealous mistress. Despised, physically mistreated, and emotionally abandoned, Hagar decided to run away from the toxic situation. Physically exhausted and emotionally spent, she collapsed by a spring in the desert. There the angel of the Lord found her; she was awakened by the angel's booming voice:

"Hagar, servant of Sarai, where have you come from and where are you going?"

"I'm running away from my mistress, Sarai," Hagar cried, covering her eyes from the angel's radiance.

The angel told her to go back and submit to her mistress, to face the situation. And then she heard the angel's blessing:

"I will so increase your descendants that they will be

too numerous to count." The angel of the Lord also said to her: "You are now with child and you will have a son. You shall name him Ishmael, for the Lord has heard your misery" (Genesis 16: 10 -11 [NIV]).

"I have seen the One who sees me!" Hagar shouted.

She named the place of the God-sighting Beer Lahai Roi. She called the Lord by the name, "El Roi—the One Who Sees Me." Hagar had experienced the presence of God and felt His comfort in a new way. El Roi saw barren Sarai convince Abram to have a child with Hagar, her Egyptian servant. El Roi saw the abuses Hagar experienced at the hands of a jealous Sarai. El Roi saw Hagar's pain and heard her cries. El Roi saw Hagar flee into the desert doomed to die. El Roi showed himself, prophesying the nation to come from the birth of her son, Ishmael. El Roi enabled Hagar to walk confidently into an insecure situation, trusting God would protect her and her unborn child.

El Roi is still "The One Who Sees Me." He sees us in our depression, desperation, abandonment, and difficulty. Maybe you don't have a break-and-run mentality like Hagar's, but if you have denied there is a problem or tried to avoid dealing with it by changing the subject, that's the same thing. Consider 2 Chronicles 16:9: "For the eyes of the Lord range throughout the earth to strengthen those whose hearts are fully committed to him" (NIV). El Roi sees and knows everything that happens to us. Hagar experienced this strengthening when she believed God's promise. We can do likewise.

Two by Two

I tried to put into practice what I was learning with MIT, but it took a new hurdle to help me connect God with real life. Our daycare provider notified me of a two-week vacation she planned for the next month, and I wondered, *What will I do? Will I need to take time off work without pay?* I knew I should commit the problem to God. But, instead, I looked inward, wished I could talk to someone, even another woman about it. It seemed as though every one of the women I knew, even the other pastors' wives were superficial friends, just mere acquaintances. I felt very alone. I headed down a rabbit trail of self-sufficiency. For two weeks, I slipped back into my old methods of worry and manipulation, as if I had completely forgotten what I had learned in MIT. I fretted as I tried to figure out a viable solution without God.

And then one morning in my prayer time, I had it out with God. I cried out about the quandary of the babysitter's vacation and my loneliness for female companionship. God showed me I needed to confess my sin of lack of trust. I felt the peace of God come over me as I read Psalm 33:18a [NIV]: "But the eyes of the Lord are on those who fear him, on those whose hope is in his unfailing love." God ministered to me in a way I had never experienced before.

"Call your sister-in-law," I sensed Him speak to my heart.

I argued, *Call my sister-in-law? Why? She doesn't babysit.*

I realized God wanted me to ask for help. But I had

built up such a wall of self-sufficiency and mistrust of people, the last thing I wanted to do was ask anyone, let alone a family member, for help. I prayed, humbled myself, and asked my sister-in-law, Sheryle Saunders, if she would be interested in babysitting Ben for the two-week vacation. She was willing. I praised God who saw and met my need for daycare and provided for our son's daily routine. This was a huge first answer to my prayer for women to walk with me through the journey of life.

Take Five

I learned how to ask El Roi for help. I also learned to nurture myself. This was one of the most difficult things for me to do. I quit several of the programs for which I had volunteered. I chose only to be involved in one that Paul worked with and one for each child. I found that to be more than adequate in staying connected with the family. "Nurturing yourself is not selfish," said message therapist Rachel Donaldson. "It actually gives you more energy and patience to manage all types of stress."

I decided to keep multitasking to a minimum. Instead of a huge list to conquer every day, I chose just two or three things each day that were realistic and tangible. I kept my calendar open, allowing for those inevitable family emergencies that would come up. I set aside about ten minutes every day for my prayer time or just to talk to another female friend by phone. Often my time of renewal was when I picked up my son from my sister-in-law's house. We'd share recipes or frustrations. We became friends through her choice to serve our family. I gained more than a babysitter—I discovered a friend, confidante, and prayer partner.

The God Who Sees

After I delivered the keynote session for a women's conference in Kitale, Kenya, an elegant, professional woman with ornately braided hair and an expensive business suit introduced herself, giving me her name, Jannice, and title. Her use of English demonstrated she was well educated and had an upper-middle-class job, yet Jannice kept her head lowered, occasionally looking up but barely making eye contact. Earlier that morning, I'd read Psalm 106:24: "Then they refused to go into the beautiful land of Canaan; they did not believe what God promised" (NCV). I prayed: "Lord, I believe You for your women to believe what You are saying to them. Help them to believe what You say." I continued to pray this way all that day, especially interceding for Jannice.

That afternoon, one of the planners set up appointments for the ladies to pray or counsel with me. Jannice was my last appointment; I knew she really needed to talk because she had waited for two hours to see me. She explained that, although she and her husband were believers, her mother-in-law had cast spells on her (Jannice's) children and was raising them as her own. I explained that the power of Jesus Christ was much greater than any spell. I reminded her that "the one who is in you is greater than the one who is in the world" (1 John 4:4 [NIV]). In our prayer time, I asked God to heal Jannice, I pleaded for Him to work in the midst of her circumstances and that she would stand up for herself and her family. I told her about El Roi, the God who sees, explaining that he sees her wherever she is; he feels her pain, and he knows her anguish. I prayed she would stand in her authority in Christ. I ended the prayer, and when I opened my eyes, she was wringing her hands and rocking back and forth. I wondered if she had really heard the prayer. I reached out and hugged her for a very long time, and we cried.

The next day, Jannice wasn't just smiling when she walked up to greet me. Jannice was glowing. She stood up straighter and taller, shoulders back, head erect, and she even made eye contact. As our eyes connected, her gaze seemed softened by belief; tears welled up and rolled down her cheeks. With excitement, we embraced and together shouted "Bwana Asifiwe!" (Praise the Lord) in celebration. This time our tears flowed with great joy as we praised God for revival.

He Sees All

Maybe you didn't fall two miles in an airplane or trek for ten days in the Amazon rainforest, but if you face your obstacles with the help of El Roi, you can know He will work all things out for good. You can be assured that our God, El Roi, sees you wherever you may be. Remember Romans 8:28: "And we know that in all things God works for the good of those who love him, who have been called according to his purpose" (NIV). Instead of running from your problems, run into the arms of El Roi. He will hold you close and give you strength to face every difficulty for His glory.

Study Questions for
Chapter 5: Alone and Afraid

1. Give the definition of abandonment as it is listed in chapter 5.

2. If you are divorced or you know someone who is, describe the feelings abandonment brings.

3. How can you use scripture to bring hope to your or someone else's circumstances?

4. Why is understanding the concept of El Roi important to those who feel abandoned?

5. Read Hagar's story in Genesis 16. Describe how she felt before and after the visit from the angel of the Lord.

6. Describe how you will call out to El Roi to meet your needs, whether they are physical, emotional, or spiritual.

6

Leveled by Loneliness

In 1944, Joe Herman was a crewmember aboard a Royal Australian Air Force bomber. The evening was peaceful, and the routine training exercise was something Herman had performed hundreds of times. He and the pilot had worked in tandem for eighteen months by this point and could almost read each other's minds. Products of thorough military training, the pair had engaged in many flawless missions, partially because of their close working relationship and effective communication. Herman's role as an assistant to the pilot in the cockpit did not include wearing a parachute. The cloudless night sky sparkled with millions of stars, a welcome backdrop for the bomber's predictable drill. Suddenly, the unthinkable happened. The bomber exploded and began to plunge downward in an uncontrollable spiral. Herman fell through the darkness amidst the debris. "This isn't happening," he thought. "An explosion wasn't part of the training exercise!" In a split second, reality hit: he was falling—without a parachute. Arms flailing wildly, he grabbed onto what he thought was a huge piece of debris. As the object slowed the speed

of his fall, Herman realized he wasn't clinging to a frag-
ment of metal wreckage but to his good friend and pilot,
John Vivash.[1]

Herman locked onto Vivash's leg in a vice-grip embrace. At that exact moment, Vivash pulled his ripcord.
Remarkably, the parachute inflated slowly, helping Herman maintain his superhero-strength grip on Vivash
through the fall to earth. Poised as a human shield, Herman hit the ground first and broke the fall of his savior,
Vivash. Vivash was alive because of his parachute, which
prevailed even with the added weight of a surprise guest.
Herman survived the perilous landing with only two broken ribs. This is amazing proof that preparation, planning,
and pairs are indispensable, especially when we launch
into the unknown.

Does Anybody Hear Me?

I stood in the church courtyard surrounded by nearly
two hundred people, and yet I felt like Herman, as though
I was falling through the air without a parachute. I was
flailing, grasping for someone to hold on to. I needed a
friend. This concept seemed strange to me. After all, my
husband was one of the pastors. If everyone knew Pastor Paul, then they should know me. I should have lots
of friends. Yet I didn't feel close to anyone. And I didn't
know much about any of the other pastors' wives, either. I
thought, *I wonder if any of them feel the same way?*

My mind drifted to earlier that Sunday morning, as
the kids and I were headed to church. I had praised God
for Paul's job. "Thank you, Lord. This is just the right fit

for his spiritual gifts." I had thanked God for the children's Bible training program. Our children, Sarah and Ben, actually looked forward to going to church now. But I noticed the friendship-void thoughts surfacing, especially after I dropped the kids off in their Sunday school classes. Crossing through the crowded church courtyard toward our adult Sunday school class, the telling reality dawned. I had no friends here. They were all at our previous church.

I noticed another pastor's wife standing on the patio, and I prayed as I walked up to her. We exchanged greetings and a bit of small talk, then, asking God for wisdom, I said, "I feel like each of us has our own church. And I don't even know you or what you do." She paused for a couple of minutes and then said, "I feel exactly the same way." After sharing our feelings, we felt connected. A pair.

I took a risk that day. It was a bold move for me to ask someone to be my friend. Sharing my feelings was scary, but the hardest part was refraining from being critical or defensive. I asked my new friend if she would mind if I put together a weekly meeting of all the pastors' wives. She suggested we ask Joyce, the senior pastor's wife, what she thought. Not only did Joyce agree that a weekly get-together would be valuable for the staff wives, but she also gave me permission to organize the time, place, and materials. Preparation, planning, and pair—plus one!

According to Craig Smith in an article on TribLIVE: "Loneliness is the number one issue impacting the wives of preachers. Their marriages are not immune to divorce and some wives, consumed by loneliness and depression, commit suicide. About 50 percent of the 2.2 million marriages in 2009 would end in divorce, according to the National Center for Health Statistics. The divorce rate among pastors is comparable. Surveys by the Global Pastors Wives Network show that 80 percent of pastors' wives feel left out and unappreciated by church members. An equal number wished their spouses would choose another profession."[2]

Soon the group of us began to meet every Friday morning. We chose my house, an early-morning time before my family was awake, and an easy curriculum to study. Most importantly, we shared life stories and scripture, laughing about life over coffee and muffins. It didn't take long for us to become part of one another's lives. It was a joy to get to know these mighty women of God, to find out more about their families and hear how to pray for them. This was a solid foundation for the beginning of new friendships.

It's Time

After several weeks of hosting the pastors' wives in my own home, my heart still felt hardened toward them. They were nice enough, genuine enough, but I simply could not allow myself to trust them. I opened the door of my home and welcomed them in, but opening the door of my heart was very difficult. I didn't want to get hurt again. While it had been two years since the last ministry, I occasionally felt the pain as if it happened last week. As if it were a dislocated joint, and when I least expected it, the thought of how the last church had shoved us out still made me wince. I remembered how much pain Paul and I had to let go of. I didn't want to go through that type of anguish again. Sour feelings of betrayal welled up in me as I categorized these women in the same way. I remembered to pray the prayer, "Dear Lord, I forgive them for making us feel like we were misunderstood and not needed. I forgive them and release them into your care."

The pastors' wives were varied in age and experience, but we had much in common: we loved the Lord, our husbands, and our families. I discovered that each woman was knowledgeable about something I needed, whether an insight about parenting, advice on how to show support to my pastor-husband, or wisdom on how to deal with difficult members of the congregation. Just as Herman clung to Vivash's leg during the free fall, I was learning to hold onto God with a little help from my new friends.

Although placing my trust in people was a concern for me, the bigger issue was God asking me to trust Him. I learned it was easier to trust the women when I was trusting God. I gave them the benefit of the doubt. Each of them wanted to draw close to God and walk the road as pastors' wives together. It became easier to trust, easier to raise my confidence, and lower my expectations, as we practiced Ecclesiastes 4:9: "Two are better than one, because they have a good return for their work" (NIV).

Loss Is Gain

Moses was known as both a friend of God and one of the greatest Jewish trailblazers in biblical history. His preparation for the role of leader of God's people began in the palace of an Egyptian pharaoh and ended with a flock of sheep in the Sinai desert. Born into a season of persecution of the Hebrew people, Moses's life was preserved when his mother sent him floating down the Nile River in a basket; Pharaoh's daughter rescued him and raised Moses as her own child (Exodus 2:5–10 [NIV]).

Moses grew up well bred, highly educated, and insulated by royal pleasures. On the day he discovered he was of Hebrew descent, he felt betrayed by his Egyptian stepparents and became confused about his identity. The reality of his heritage confirmed his opinions and feelings about the evil society ruled by Pharaoh. For years Moses had witnessed with disgust and mistrust the Egyptians' repeated mistreatment of the Hebrew slaves. Now he took it personally, as the Hebrews were his relatives. The result: Moses would plummet headlong into an act that would forever change history.

Moses's life was marked by his responses to circumstances. While still under his stepfather Pharaoh's marble roof, Moses jumped into a fight to defend a Hebrew slave and killed an Egyptian (Exodus 2:12 [NIV]). Moses chose to run from the consequences of murder and left Egypt, preferring certain death in the desert to punishment by Pharaoh. Instead, Moses found peace and refuge in Midian, where he settled into life as an immigrant husband, father, and shepherd (Exodus 2:15–21 [NIV]).

At first glance, one might think Moses got second best. Everything changed as he fled the comforts of the palace, familiar surroundings, and the provision of his surrogate Egyptian family. Moses became a stranger in a strange land, an experience that God used to prepare him for leadership. In Exodus 3:2, God offers himself to Moses: "There the angel of the Lord appeared to him in flames of fire from a burning bush. Moses saw though the bush was on fire, it didn't burn up. Moses thought, 'I will go over and see this strange sight—why the bush does not burn up.' God called to him from the burning bush, 'Moses, Moses!'" (NIV). This was Moses's first encounter with God's nearness and presence as his friend.

Holy Ground

Moses's burning bush experience happened while he was tending his flocks in the Midian fields. My burning bush experience happened the day I tended the flocks on the crowded church courtyard. Moses drew near to God and made a choice to listen to His voice. I heard God's voice over the din of the crowd. I listened as I chose to reach out. God showed me my need, and He also gave me a plan. I could have argued with God like Moses did when God called him into ministry. I could have made up a bunch of excuses and reasons why the plan might not work.

Instead, I chose to act and even risk rejection. I am thankful I did. The pastors' wives' group took preparation, planning, and prayer. My time of loneliness prepared me to minister with compassion to pastors' wives who might not want to admit their lack of friends. It made the difference in my life and in the lives of many other women. In time, the women provided the counsel I needed to leave my full-time job to be available at home for my children and assist in Pastor Paul's ministry. In fact, my time with the other wives flourished, linking me with opportunities to minister to yet more pastors' wives across our county and ultimately opening a door for me to write a monthly column for *Focus on the Family Pastors' Family* magazine specifically targeting pastors' wives. I wrote my column for four years, sharing many of the lessons I had learned from the other wives, as well as truths I learned from His word. Ultimately, God gave me a heart for leaders and showed me the importance of the role of a pastor's wife—its influence, loneliness, mystery, and responsibility. A pastor's wife can either make or break his ministry.

I Am Every Woman

It has been my honor to share my story for God's glory when I have spoken at conferences and to pastors' wives and women's groups around the world. Many people think speakers like me have no problems. To set the record straight, I tell my story to level the playing field. I am a woman with struggles, just like each one in the crowd. Although my struggles may be different and vary in intensity, we all face trials as well as victories being a part of the human race.

In one of the themed women's retreats, I present the opening message, "My Heart's Desire." In it I explain that we are the very longing of the heart of Jesus and that He loves us with an everlasting love (Jeremiah 31:3). I am an example of how the intimate passion of Jesus can rescue someone from a life of physical, emotional, and mental addictions. My life message is an opportunity for women to not only hear about God's transforming power but also take me off the perfection pedestal.

Years after graduating from Bible school, my spiritual growth had remained stunted. Despite being married to a pastor, serving the Lord, reading the Bible, and participating in prayer groups, I still couldn't forgive myself for the sins I had committed twenty years before. Relief came when I finally fully trusted God's love to cover my multitude of sins. I accepted God's forgiveness and let go of the blame, shame, and low self-worth that had been sucking the life out of me. It's always a gift for me to remind myself of God's power. "He reached down from on high and took hold of me; he drew me out of deep waters. He rescued me from my powerful enemy, from my foes, who were too strong for me. They confronted me in the day of my disaster, but the Lord was my support. He brought me out into a spacious place; he rescued me because he delighted in me" (Psalm 18:16–19 [NIV]).

I weave my story together with the truths of identity in Christ; I share how God renewed my mind through His word. Since understanding our identities in Christ is absolutely essential to our success at living the victorious Christian life, we must get this before we will see real change in how we behave. Usually by this point in my speech there are unanimous nods of agreement and at least one or two resounding shouts of amen from the audience.

Evelyn's Story

I was the keynote speaker for a women's retreat in Southern California. In the first session, near the end of the "My Heart's Desire" message, my eyes scanned the eager women's faces, thankful to see them hungry for more truth. Most of the women's eyes revealed expressions of relief. However, one woman in particular barely made eye contact with me, and, when she did, her eyes were full of agony, skepticism, and mistrust. I was taken aback by her expression of sad hopelessness. The Holy Spirit's direction helped me feel her pain; I prayed for her, although I hadn't met her. I knew that God would show me how He wanted to bear her burdens. She heard my story and His longing for her heart to be healed and whole emotionally. She wanted the same thing for herself, but was unable to accept that God wanted healing for her. Evelyn hadn't planned for God to open her heart to a new level of friendship with him. I approached Evelyn after the session, "Come by my room tomorrow afternoon and let's talk."

The next evening, Evelyn stopped by and haltingly said, "I came by your room today and you weren't there." "I'm sorry," I said. "It must have been when I went out to get something to drink. Let's try again, after the evening session." As I turned away, I prayed, "Lord let her trust me. Lord, help her to trust You." I knew Evelyn was testing God and me by the way she acted as if we didn't really care about her.

After the evening session on forgiveness, Evelyn stayed behind so she and I could talk. We decided to sit in the hot tub. At the edge of the pool, we soaked our weary bare feet and bore our spiritual souls. She took me on a short life journey, a place she apparently didn't like to go. In elementary school, she became a pleaser; her key relationships were based on presentation. At an early age, she strove for high achievement, hiding her true feelings and performing better than everyone else. A long-distance runner in high school, she remained competitive. To keep her weight down, she developed anorexia nervosa. When she met her future husband, then a youth pastor, the relationship was about a continued front she had to maintain in his presence. She found herself falling apart when he wasn't around. Now married to the youth pastor, she still felt as if she had to keep up the front. To add to the mix, Evelyn hadn't grieved the death of her mother from breast cancer. These issues and more were the meat of our conversation. I shared with Evelyn God's passion for her. His love was not dependent on her performance. Her part was simply to receive everything God had for her.

Here's a card I received from Evelyn on Mother's Day:

For Someone Who's Always Close To My Heart—The special people in our lives touch our days with joy, fill our hearts with gratitude, and share love with open arms. And then on the inside: But whatever the special quality is, it makes you a unique and wonderful person and that's why you mean so much to me. In her handwriting: Sheryl, Happy Mother's Day! I am not sure where I would be if you hadn't approached me. Your love broke through the walls of disappointment and grief that were around my broken heart. God used you to begin to heal my heart—I am sure of that!

God's love for Evelyn is how God loves you. Maybe you are grasping for something or someone to grip. Perhaps you feel as if you are falling without a parachute. God wants you to reach out for Him and hold on tight.

God fully provided for Evelyn. He fully provided for Moses. In fact, scripture records that Moses was known as a friend of God.

"The Lord would speak to Moses face to face, as a man speaks with his friend" (Exodus 33:11 [NIV]). God shaped Moses's outstanding personality. God did not change what or who Moses was. Instead, he took Moses's characteristics and molded them until they were suited to His purposes. God wants to do the same thing with us. He can and will use each and every situation if we let Him. If we use a little preparation and planning and work in pairs, God will strengthen us.

Study Questions for
Chapter 6: Leveled by Loneliness

1. Explain a time in your life when you felt like you were falling without a parachute.

2. Give details about the feelings you experienced.

3. Have you ever shared these feelings with another person? Would you take a risk and share these feelings with God?

4. In the past, if you have grasped onto something or someone other than what is good for you, explain your journey.

5. Expound on the concept of a friendship with God. Describe what it means to you and how it affects your friendships with your friends, husband, children, and family members.

Piled in a Heap

James Boole, an extreme sports lover from Tamworth, survived a 6,000-foot fall without a parachute. The thirty-one-year-old hit rocks at an estimate 100 kilometers per hour. His chute launched only seconds to the ground, and Boole landed on snow-covered rocks. For a split second, he lay piled in a heap, unable to move his mangled body. Amazingly, Boole survived, suffering only a broken rib and back.[1] Change interrupts our lives in much the same way—we find ourselves in midair, scrambling to put the brakes on in an attempt to stop the inevitable.

Change is in the Air

Change might feel out of control; no way to stop the free-fall, but one can survive. Jill Briscoe said,[2] "Change interrupts our nesting habits and intrudes into my comfort zone. But with each change we have a new start, a clean page, and an opportunity to try again. That hope renews us." So a relaxed summer schedule was a welcome relief for me as a home-school mom. In my fifth year of home schooling, I looked forward to a break from the regimen of homework, strict bedtimes, and our young family's project deadline calendar. Although our little family of four worked together in harmony without much effort or strife, it felt good to actually enjoy spending time with each other. We looked ahead to summertime fun.

Thankfully, we got through the school year famously—science projects, oral language, and even a California missions project. We collaborated together to take field trips, do research at the library, and made fun ventures to the craft store. Who would have thought that, years prior, I considered fleeing my precious loved ones because of my emotional pain? Just like hundreds of women, I came within a sneeze of bailing out on my responsibilities. I shuddered at the thought that I might have gone AWOL on the responsibility of parenting and being a pastor's wife. I thanked God, how in His mercy and perfect timing. He saw fit to connect me with like-minded women friends.

Spiritually, I experienced freedom like I'd never known. My mind remained clear from thoughts of unworthiness; I had few pangs of guilt and even fewer incidences of remembering things that brought me shame. I understood how to walk in my identity in Christ. I quoted the "In Christ I Am" list as often as necessary. Memorizing scripture was not easy for me, yet every day I wrote a Scripture on a 3-x-5 card to have as a handy reminder of God's presence.

A few months prior to the end of the school year, I'd found my niche serving in our county as a conference director. I worked year-round with a team of volunteers to seek out keynote speakers, recruit seminar leaders, exhibitors, and other amenities to organize a lay-training event for the local churches. What a joy for me to work with this bunch of energetic believers whose focal point was to find ways to strengthen the body of Christ.

As my God-confidence increased, my self-confidence rose to new levels. I received numerous speaking invitations to share my story. *Public speaking? Me? Had God chosen the wrong girl?* I discussed my fears and concerns with Paul, who said, "You are a natural speaker." I didn't feel that way—Paul made public speaking look so easy; he was the one who was the "natural." I later learned that he worked at it through preparation, which made public speaking look easy. His comfortable style invited the audience into his world. Paul became my public speaking coach and audience for live practice.

In addition to leading the spring Christian leadership-training convention and emceeing the event, I taught a women's seminar and exhibited my writing and speaking ministry. A representative from KAXL 88.3 Life FM radio read my *Kindred Moments Newsletter for Pastor's Wives and Women in Ministry.* I was pleasantly surprised when she asked me if I had ever written anything for radio. I said no. She asked if I would like to try writing and recording radio scripts. Excited and challenged, I was pleased for yet another opportunity, a media method, for sharing the truths God impressed on my heart. My short feature, *Kindred Moments with Sheryl Giesbrecht*, began a short time later. It was a blessing and a challenge for me to allow God's help in this endeavor. It is amazing how many spiritual truths can be shared in thirty seconds to two minutes.

Excited about a more flexible summer schedule, I looked forward to increased opportunities to write devotionals, magazine articles, and radio scripts. I planned longer times of Bible study in the mornings, so when I began to write, there would be something worthwhile to say. Each morning was like Christmas. I eagerly went to my quiet time, full of anticipation for new ways God would show me how to unwrap His gifts as we sat in our time together. Thankfully, God had given me His bounty. When the unwelcome hurricane of change stormed in to rearrange our lives, I was studied up and prayed up.

The Wind Changes

Our world is in constant flux—the stock market rises and falls, the weather is too hot or too cold, we change our minds, our fashion tastes and even our weight changes. There's a saying: "The only thing constant in life is change." We must expect change and count on it to happen, but dealing with it is usually not much fun. I am a creature of habit. I like my routine. Beth Moore said, "I get so comfortable in my rut, I hang up pictures in there."[3] I agree with Moore. I don't like change.

The Squall Rises

My son Ben was an intelligent and self-motivated twelve-year-old, essential qualities for a youngster in home school. However, he typically finished his schoolwork early and grew easily bored. I felt he needed socializing outside of what our church and I could provide. The local city school district offered services to home-school parents, which included master teachers, a curriculum, and classes on local school campuses. I enrolled Ben in an art class and in band. These two opportunities provided both of us with the connections we needed. Ben's perseverance during his sixth-grade year marked a decision for me to enroll him in public school for seventh grade. Participation in the band happened during the literal calendar of the school year. Art classes took place during the summer. This decision to send Ben to public school for the seventh grade in the fall marked yet another change for our family unit.

Paul's ministry focus at church had changed. Within two years in college ministry he led numerous mission trips, enlarging his heart for unreached people groups. (www.JoshuaProject.org) He and a good friend prayed through the 10/40 window, leading young lives and our church body to do the same. It was an amazing time of spiritual growth along with cultural awareness for our little family and the church we served.

Paul's heart was increasingly drawn to serving outside of the United States. He was willing to go, and I was willing to send him. But when Paul asked me whether I would approve him joining with his good friend as a ministry partner to actually launch out on their own as missionaries, my initial answer was "no."

Paul asked me to pray about it. I prayed through the decision. Ultimately I knew the choice was Paul's. When Paul told me he was going to start an international organization, I had reservations, but knew I had no choice but to support him. The ministry sustained strong momentum for many months, but then Paul and I noticed changes in leadership attitudes of the supporting church. We found out his ministry partner had made major changes Paul knew nothing about. He was no longer a board member, a bank signer, nor did he have access to money that was donated for a major project. Paul was without a job.

Paul had been on staff for eight of the twelve years we attended this church, and we were their missionaries. Paul and I joined forces in prayer; we met with the church staff. We gathered a group, which included Paul's ministry partner and a mediator, who suggested scriptural intervention for churches with difficulties, but to no avail. We knew God was moving us on, again. Like Abraham who, by faith stepped out into God's plan, we, too, left a job and a ministry family—we didn't know where we were going. "Abraham went out, not knowing where he was going" (Hebrews 11:8 [NIV]). We really could relate—storm numbers one, two, and three: a child changed schools, no job, and no church.

The Torrent Ensues

One afternoon as I worked in my kitchen, the cell phone buzzed. I picked up the call, recognizing the familiar voice of Paul's friend Randall. He sounded upset. "Paul has been in a motorcycle accident. He's coming home, but I am not sure if he's okay." I paced frantically, wanting to find Paul, but I didn't know where he'd been riding. I felt helpless and began to pray. Within an hour, Paul came home, covered in dirt, clothes torn, and his elbows and forehead scraped. He assured me he was okay.

He explained how he rode in new territory and took an unfamiliar turn. The front tire hit the soft dirt; he overcorrected and flipped the motorcycle. Thankfully, he landed on his shoulder not his head. A trip to the emergency room showed a broken scapula. This was not good news for our family at the beginning of the summer; it ruined our summer plans for fun. However, the news was devastating for Pastor Paul who was at the beginning of a job search.

Captives of Change

The Babylonians took the children of Israel as prisoners into slavery. Jeremiah wrote a letter telling them to move ahead with their lives and pray for the pagan nation that enslaved them. This seemed like strange advice. Pray for your captors?

"This is what the Lord Almighty, the God of Israel, says to all those I carried into exile from Jerusalem to Babylon: Build houses settle down; and eat what they produce. Marry and have sons and daughters; find wives from your sons and give your daughters in marriage, so that they, too, may have sons and daughters. Increase in number there; do not decrease. Also, seek the peace and prosperity of the city to which I have carried you into exile. Pray to the Lord for it, because if it prospers, you, too, will prosper" (Jeremiah 29:4–23 [NIV]).

The children of Israel were taken by force into a pagan, enemy nation, and yet the prophet Jeremiah told them to pray for the city. He explained, "If you pray for that which has taken you captive, if it prospers, you will also prosper." This doesn't mean that we should ask God to change our circumstances, to get us out of the mess we are in. But it does mean we should ask God how we can pray for the change that has taken us captive and allow God to teach us what He has for us to learn in the midst of it.

Our circumstances might take us by surprise and force us to face a foe we'd rather avoid. But with the interruption of change, God is never surprised. Life brings us changes through disease: fibromyalgia, cancer, HIV, and AIDS. Another change is denial or doubt—it's the person who says, "I don't believe, God." Depression is another challenge we might have to face—it's the person who says, "I am piled in a heap and can't get up." Or there's the change of destruction—9/11, Hurricane Katrina, or China's earthquakes. Another interruption is despair—the person who asks, "Why am I here?" Or the change of divorce—you might say, "He left me; I am abandoned, alone. It wasn't my plan to be divorced. I thought he would take care of me forever." Or there's the change of discouragement. The best explanation for this is the person who says, "I can't go on." Unfortunately, we must talk about the change of domestic violence, more common in our church settings than we'd like to admit. It's often called the "silent suffering." There are many other changes and challenges we face, but the last one I would like to note is the change of death— the loss of a grandparent, parent, spouse, or child. Each of these issues brings layers of losses that must be dealt with. H. Norman Wright, in his book *Recovering from the Losses in Life*, said, "It is vital that you identify every loss in your life for what it is—a loss—and then grieve for it, just as you would for someone who died."[4]

No matter how distressing or unpleasant a situation is,

we must keep moving and adjust to it. We often find this difficult to do. Our response might be anything other than to pray for the change that has taken us prisoner. We usually want to fix the problem, worry about it, or run from it. But God's admonition found in I Timothy 2:1, 2 says: "I urge, then, first of all, that requests, prayers, intercession and thanksgiving be made for everyone—for kings and all those in authority, that we may live peaceful and quiet lives in all godliness and holiness" (NIV).

The Eye of the Hurricane

I was in a tailspin—Ben was changing schools, Paul was without a job, our family was church hunting, and now Paul had a broken scapula. I remembered my Mom's in Touch group's verses on the unchanging attribute of God. God's plan for us in the challenge of change is to find His stability and rely on this character quality of his nature—His immutability. God does not change; it's His character to remain the same. "In the beginning, you laid the foundations of the earth, but you remain the same and your years never end" (Psalm 102:25–27 [NIV]). God does not and will not change. Our feeble human minds can't fathom what that means. When we anticipate change and, dare I say, become at home with change, we can show the world how to live.

Jeremiah 29:7 reminded me to "seek the peace and prosperity of the city to which I have carried you into exile. Pray to the Lord for it, because if it prospers, you, too, will prosper" (NIV). How could I seek the peace and prosperity of the enemy city of Ben leaving home school to attend public school? I prayed, "Lord show me Your will. You have directed this decision, and I ask for the peace and Your prosperity in this change." How could I find peace in the antagonistic situation of Paul's job loss or the hostile feelings of the loss of our church family? My prayer continued, "God I ask for your presence in this battle of leaving the church we have grown to love. Heal our family. Take us into new territory. I seek the peace and prosperity of this situation, although I feel disconnected and betrayed. I ask for Your hand of blessing to rule over our family." Finally, the frosting on the cake of our trial was Paul's broken scapula. I prayed, "Lord, how could this be? My husband is looking for a job, and now he is laid out flat on the couch. I ask for your peace and prosperity in the enemy territory of broken bones and foiled dreams."

My circumstances leveled me. I was piled in a heap of change. Feelings of doubt of God's love coupled with discouragement and distrust of God's people caused me to be overwhelmed. These prayers of commitment became my daily mantra. I sought peace and prosperity of the enemies of discouragement, doubt, and despair that had captured me. I would not let these enemies rule. I chose to trust God, reminded how I'd implemented the steps of forgiveness toward my brothers and sisters who wronged us. I had fully forgiven them. And now using the same process, I chose to forgive the circumstances surrounding Ben's school change, which had made me feel out of control. I forgave Paul for riding the motorcycle. I grasped the promise God gave to the captives in Babylon found in Jeremiah 29:11–12, "For I know the plans I have for you, declares the Lord, plans to prosper you and not to harm you, plans to give you hope and a future. Then you will call upon me and pray to me and I will listen to you. You will seek me and find me when you seek me with all of your heart. I will be found by you, declares the Lord, I will bring you back from captivity" (NIV).

Linda's Story

The evening I heard Sheryl speak on change was a gift from God. Just months before, my husband lost his job; I had to go back to work full-time, which meant the kids were now in daycare. Sheryl told the story of Jeremiah 29:4–12, urging me to pray for the peace and prosperity of the change that was keeping me captive. It changed my life for the better. I admitted before God my resentment about our situation. As I confessed my sin, the anger dissipated, the clouds of frustration lifted. I also learned how to grieve the loss of being a full-time stay-at-home mom, and gave up control of my husband as the bread-winner. I am finally free from the captivity of change. I know how to stay free.

The Lord's freedom has been declared for all of us. Whatever change comes our way, we can let go of the familiar and embrace something new. We will no longer find ourselves piled in a heap. We are free to get back up, stand tall, and walk in freedom in Christ.

Study Questions for
Chapter 7: Piled in a Heap

1. Describe a time of change in your life.

2. Explain a coping mechanism you used to navigate your way through change.

3. Expound on the attribute of the immutability of God.

4. Share a new coping mechanism you learned from this lesson.

5. Describe how you might tell someone else how God set you free from captivity.

8

Tripped up over Technology

Bahia Bakari and her mother were traveling by airplane from their home in Paris, France, for a summer vacation in Comoros when the improbable happened. An engine malfunction caused Airbus A310, Yemenia Flight 626, to crash into the Indian Ocean near the north coast of Grande Comore, Comoros, killing all other 152 people on board. Bakari, who could barely swim and had no life vest, clung to aircraft wreckage, floating in heavy seas for more than thirteen hours, much of it in pitch darkness, before being rescued.

Bakari was sighted by the *Sima Com 2*, a privately owned ship. She was thrown a life preserver, but the waters were too rough, and she was too exhausted to grab it. One of the sailors jumped into the water and handed her a flotation device, after which they were both pulled safely aboard the *Sima Com 2*. Bakari was given dry blankets and a hot drink. This fortunate French school girl became world famous as the sole survivor of Yemenia Flight 626.[1]

Circle of Life

Paul's physical healing from the motorcycle injuries took about a year, but more important was the emotional healing he received from the previous ministry departure. After the accident, per doctor's orders, he spent the summer recuperating. He stayed down flat, with his right forearm and shoulder in an immobilizing brace, making it impossible to lift or write. He proved a good patient and did what the doctor ordered.

I spent the summer as the mom-taxi, taking the kids back and forth to swim lessons, vacation Bible school, and play dates with friends. I remember one sticky summer morning, a few days after the accident, the kids and I were packed up and ready to head out the door for swimming. We stopped by the living room couch where Paul was camped. The kids and I laid hands on him and prayed. As we finished, I said, "I think God wants you to spend the summer praying about your next ministry." Paul said, "I think you are right."

In the midst of Paul's summer of recovering from his physical and emotional brokenness, we grew closer as a family. We finally had time together. I felt relief from the whole concept of sharing Paul with the church and his ministry. It was liberating to be free from church responsibilities and programs. Although we missed the people in our ministry, our weekends were open to spending more time together as a family. Paul and I hadn't realized how much fun it would be to spend time away from town with the kids on a weekend trip. Now we had Saturday and

Sunday off, like regular people. We hardly knew how to act.

The four of us found a local church near our house, with a service on Saturday nights. We liked the casual feel, and the music was comfortable, too. Paul and I had become acquainted with the senior pastor through community involvements. We liked his preaching. My middle-school-aged kids liked the surroundings, too, and were even making new friends. Everything seemed to be settling into place, except for one thing—Paul was still looking for a job. He wasn't sure if he wanted another job in a ministry position. Like a united front, we prayed together as a family over what God's will was for us.

Falling into Faith

The planning committee for the Christian Ministry Convention held regular meetings year-round. Paul and I were a team. Even with the planning of the conventions, we worked side by side. As I led the team, he filled in where it was needed, which was usually logistics and facility management. One of our meetings was on the campus of our new church, since we were considering the campus as an option for our next convention's host church. Paul and I walked down the hallway of the expansive campus, heading to our meeting room. We saw the pastor heading into the other direction and shouted out a greeting to him. He said, "Oh hi, Paul, it's good to see you—by the way I have a position open if you are interested." Paul and I looked at each other and knew God was working. We were excited.

Paul set up a meeting with the pastor for the next

week. We prayed together, and our anticipation for what lay ahead increased. We decided we were done playing church. This season of change was a newfound release from church routines; it had showed us a lot about what we were becoming. We had been too busy for our family and even too busy for God. In the process of Paul's healing, we slowed down, got to know each other, and grew familiar with self-examination. We discovered we had become dishonest in many areas.

For me, it was a lack of focus on the family and the finances. I found myself wanting more and more time alone—to write and remain in prayer. I went away for the weekend once a month, totally alone, to write and meditate. Although these were good things, my time became increasingly self-focused instead of God-focused. I grew increasingly selfish.

Paul's struggle began at age four, when he had been exposed to pornography. The first incident seared images in his mind that remained distractions even at a young age. During grade school and junior high, he was curious and picked up a few *Playboy* magazines from the trash bins. Throughout high school, he continued to struggle, keeping his demons at bay through scripture memory and Christian music. In college, his inquisitiveness won when he was exposed to the Internet. It was too easy to access— Paul had fallen headlong into the pit of Internet pornography.

Put in a Pit

Joseph's pit was of a different sort. You may remember hearing his story in Sunday school. Joseph was the next to the youngest of twelve brothers, whose adoring father Jacob showed him preference and gave him a robe—"a coat of many colors." The robe became a symbol of his father's favoritism toward Joseph, aggravating strained relations between Joseph and his brothers.

Joseph's literal free-fall took place when, in their rage, his jealous older brothers plotted his death and pushed him into a well. "So when Joseph came to his brothers, they stripped him of the richly ornamented robe he was wearing—and they took him and threw him into the cistern" (Genesis 37:23 [NIV]). Joseph was betrayed and deserted by his family, yet God's providence and hand of protection provided rescue. Reuben talked Joseph's brothers out of killing him. Midian merchants ventured near the well where Joseph had been placed; the brothers seized an opportunity to rid themselves of Joseph once and for all—without killing him themselves. Joseph's own family sold him into slavery.

Circumstances of victimization can cause us to fall into a pit of survival behavior, which could lead to our spiritual demise. These things are often beyond our control—a job promotion given to someone else when it was our turn, overlooked at family gatherings, misunderstood by people we love and trust. Children who have been abused have much to overcome. Their ill-treatment can open the door for future obsessive/compulsive behaviors. Drug addicts and alcoholics understand the draw of dependence and compulsion for more—it sucks them into a place of obligation to the flesh. Pornography addiction is a pit fashioned by our own cravings and can become a spiritual graveyard.

The statistics of the impact of pornography on our culture is depressing. In the United States, 70 to 80 percent of Christian men say they are, "addicted at some level." Women say this same tendency is true for them as well. Shockingly, most children are exposed and using porn by the age of fourteen. For young adults, it's too late for focus on planning strategies because the person has already fallen into the pit of pornography and may never get out.

Our church and culture has been poisoned by pornography. This means many of us are in recovery from pornography. When we are honest and bring the secret into the light, recovery begins. "Into the light" means acknowledging to others that we are struggling with the effects of this problem.

"It is God's will that you should be sanctified: that you should avoid sexual immorality; that each of you should learn to control his own body in a way that is holy and honorable, not in passionate lust like the heathen" (I Thessalonians 4:3–5 [NIV]). Imagine if we avoided pornography altogether? Instead of talking about it, spending time discussing it in counseling, and focusing on it over and over again, what if we learned control? Control is God's will.

Proper Response

Joseph's responses marked his public and private integrity. As a boy he was betrayed and deserted by his family. As a young man he was exposed to sexual temptation when the wife of Potiphar, a chief official to Pharaoh, flirted with him. While serving a long prison sentence for a crime he did not commit, he was forgotten. Joseph didn't spend much time asking "Why?" but used the approach "What shall I do now?" Joseph's public life and private integrity were the same. He acknowledged God's presence with him. He included God in all of his plans, and, even when circumstances seemed bleak, he practiced self-control and kept close to the Lord.

God's hand of favor remained on Joseph during his life and prison sentence. So when the cup-bearer needed a dream interpreted, Joseph's reputation surfaced, and Joseph was given the opportunity to do so. In Genesis 40:8, Joseph said, "Do not interpretations belong to God? Tell me your dreams" (NIV). Again Joseph was forgotten for another two years. Then Pharaoh needed a dream interpreted. God showed Joseph favor. Even Pharaoh noticed Joseph's spirit. "Can we find anyone like this man in whom is the Spirit of God?" (Genesis 41:38 [NIV]).

A Bottomless Pit

Of course, we are to avoid pornography, but the bigger issue is learning to control our bodies. Joseph chose to control himself. Potiphar's wife had flirted with him. He rebuked her advances. For people who enter the church with pornography in their backgrounds, teaching them to avoid it often comes too late. The only way to help them is to offer a safe place based on confession and accountability with support.

Recovery from the effects of pornography is not a one-time treatment. It is not a pill we take, a book we read, or therapy we undergo just once. It's a discipline that is never finished. Recovery is a lifelong call to holiness, seeking to replace the memories, images, and lusts of inappropriate sexual content with holy thoughts and images of biblical truth. Is this possible? Of course. But it requires a constant commitment to personal purity and accountability to someone else. We can't fight pornography alone.

How to Pull Yourself Out of the Pit of Pornography[2]

1. Commit to your own personal purity, no matter the cost. Coming clean may have a significant impact on our marriages and families, not to mention our ministries and ourselves—but it is something we must do.

2. Find a few people who will walk alongside you. These must be people to whom you can be accountable and who will keep asking the hard questions. They become your confidantes, confronters, and encouragers.

3. Begin a lifelong journey of following Jesus with all of your thoughts and feelings. What we watch comes out of our thoughts, by which I mean that our thinking usually serves to drive us toward activities. If we are thinking impure thoughts, we will be drawn to impure actions.

Acceptance and Accountability

Sexual sin is an abomination to God. We need to state it for what it is. In our culture, we have become desensitized to sexual sin, especially in our thought life. In Leviticus 11:44, God commanded, "Be holy because I am holy" (NIV). Whether it is in our thoughts or in our actions, God would not have given this commandment if it were impossible to keep. Satan's power over us is in the secret places. If we keep our sexual thoughts, desires, and urges to ourselves, we are leaving the door open for the evil one to create lies and distortion.

Jody's Story

Thank you for sharing your story about Paul's addiction to pornography. I thought I was the only woman in the world whose husband struggled with an internet addiction. I've felt so alone, betrayed, insecure, and deceived. My prayers have finally been answered. I now know my husband's addiction is not my fault; it's been such a huge issue for us through the years, I've always been blamed for our unsatisfying sex life. Thank you for giving me confidence that God cares about my marriage.

I am thankful for the tools you shared to help me realign my identity in Christ. I am so grateful. I praise God for you!

Climbing Out

A few weeks later, Paul accepted the pastoral position at our new church. It was a good fit. With God's tender loving care, he was honest with himself and me. Although years of resentment had built up, I offered acceptance and unconditional love. I used the prayer of forgiveness and pardoned Paul for betraying the family and me. I chose to trust him once again. He chose accountability with a few close male friends. He came to grips with the areas in which he needed healing and preached his first sermon on his struggle with pornography.

From that time, Paul hosted men's accountability groups and encouraged them to be honest with God and each other. Paul's influence was far-reaching and needed, since many men's groups avoided the topic altogether. Sexual sin has been around a long time, and we need to see the whole of biblical history as the arena where people dealt with sexual sin and got on with life. Freedom from sexual bondage brings freedom from oppressed feelings, a life of integrity, and a connection with our divine Lord in a new and glorious way.

Study Questions for
Chapter 8: Tripped up over Technology

1. Did you learn anything new about the statistics of pornography?

2. Describe a few of the effects of pornography.

3. Joseph was placed into a pit. How did his attitude help him to get out?

4. List the ways to pull yourself out of the pit of pornography.

5. How did the author's husband allow God to use his struggle for God's glory?

Flat on My Face

In March of 1985 Dave Hodgman jumped at 12,000 feet as part of an assembly of skydivers attempting to build a formation in the skies over Victoria, Australia. He was unable to reach the group. When he opened his parachute at around 2,500 feet, he had not realized he was below another jumper, who also did not realize Hodgman was there. The other jumper, Frank, was just opening his own chute at the time. He collided with Hodgman, knocking him out and becoming entangled in his lines. The two men came down together under Frank's inflated chute and Hodgman's chute, which had collapsed and re-inflated through the entire ride. Frank had no control, and the two came down between some cars in a packed-gravel parking lot. Hodgman was badly injured but returned to jumping within three months. Although he had fallen flat on his face onto a parking lot, he survived because his lines had become entangled with another parachute, which replaced his failed chute.[1]

The Discovery

Life at our new ministry settled into a favorable routine for our family. Paul's choice to remain open and honest with his pornography struggles had affected the family in many positive ways, bringing healing to our marriage. Paul's honesty at church was refreshing to many men who struggled with the same addiction to internet pornography. In the first sermon Paul preached, he said he chose accountability and honesty to the point he would face his computer screen to an outside window. He wanted everyone at the church to know he had nothing to hide. Paul continued to share his victories, and God blessed him. Our love increased for the body of Christ at our new church. We served God together and team-taught side by side in an adult Sunday school class.

One morning, I was putting on my makeup and found a lump underneath my left eye. Thinking it was an allergic reaction, I took some medicine and changed my brand of eye makeup. A few weeks later, when the lump was considerably larger—now blocking my vision—a doctor referred me to a specialist. In the weeks that followed, those specialists looked for answers through mysterious and uncomfortable tests.

From Fear To ...

Fear is an emotional response to an unknown future or uncomfortable situation. But fear can also cause us to doubt God and His provision, opening up the door for defense mechanisms such as self-pity, discouragement, anger, and even depression. The Hebrew word for fear is *pachad*, meaning to tremble, to be in trepidation, to be on one's guard or to have terror. Fear happens when we feel out of control. Fear is a natural response to danger—like when an animal hears a loud sound that startles them and they break and run. This is *pachad*.

"Keep your eyes closed and hold very still," the X-ray technician instructed while the table I was laying on slid into the coffin-like MRI tube. Velcro-strapped onto the examination table, I really had no choice but to do as I was told. On the outside, I was motionless. But on the inside, my mind was exploding. *What if I have a brain tumor? They only do MRIs if they suspect something is really serious. I must have something life-threatening.*

Inside the claustrophobic tube, the ultraviolet X-ray lights slowly scanned my head millimeter by millimeter. My mind raced through a gamut of questions. *God, what is going on? Why is this happening to me? What is the lump?* I knew I would have to get control of myself or the three-hour test might not be completed because this patient was going berserk. Fear overwhelmed my senses. In the MRI tube, I was told not to move my mouth, so singing or praying aloud during the ordeal was out of the question. My unsettled mind reached out, "Help me, Lord," I shuddered silently as the test drug on. I remembered studying Psalm 27:1 that morning, "The Lord is my light and my salvation—whom shall I fear? The Lord is the stronghold of my life—of whom shall I be afraid?" (NIV) God's truth and peace comforted me as I realized I had nothing to fear—not MRI claustrophobia, the mysterious tests, the uncertain diagnosis, the imminent treatment. Not even the unknown future. I moved through my fear and into the confidence of God's provision and protection that overrides the feeling of fear. We don't know what our future holds, but God does. We let God be God when, by faith, we actually trust Him as the God of our future. We can walk into the uncertainties and the unknowns trusting He is already there, waiting for us. "Surely God is my salvation; I will trust and not be afraid" (Isaiah 12:2 [NIV]). Someone once said, "I do not know what the future holds, but I know who holds the future."

The MRI test showed a lump contained in the lower part of the lymph nodes of the eyelid. At least it wasn't a brain tumor. The doctors recommended a biopsy of the lump. You can imagine our shock when Paul and I heard the opthalmologist's review of the biopsy results: You have lymphoma, cancer.

A couple of days after the appointment, it was Sunday morning. The black cloud of the recent cancer diagnosis hung over my head. Our church prayer quilting team asked people to tie a knot and say a prayer for me. As I headed out of the sanctuary doors, prayer quilt under my arm, someone handed me a book by Dr. David Jeremiah, who had two bouts with cancer. *Kindred Moments with Sheryl Giesbrecht* was the name of my show on Christian radio, but in Dr. Jeremiah's book, *A Bend in the Road*, I found out about another type of moment—*a disruptive moment*.

Disruptive moments are often divine appointments. 2 Corinthians 12 identifies Satan as the messenger sent to test and torment Paul. But the devil wasn't given free reign. He couldn't do anything to Paul that God wouldn't allow. The moment we accept the fact that our ordeal has been permitted, even intended by God, our perspective on disruptive moments will totally change. We find ourselves saying, "God, You have allowed this in my life. I don't understand it, but I know that it couldn't have happened to me unless it was filtered through your loving hands. So this thing is from you."[2]

No, God didn't cause this thing to happen to me; He allowed it for His glory. None of us welcome suffering, but once we have gone through it, we can offer comfort in a way we could not have before. C.S. Lewis said, "Suffering is what drives us out of the nursery into the world of others."[3] As believers, we may feel we should be exempt from trials, but we know that "the rain falls on the just and the unjust," and we are not excluded from the good or the bad.

My desire during the whole cancer experience was that God would be glorified. However, when we were shown results of the PET scan, we were in disbelief—the cancer not only was in the lymph node of my left eyelid, but it was in the bone marrow of my right arm, shoulder and elbow, and in the femur of my left leg. I was told I had stage-four, non-Hodgkin's lymphoma. I had cancer in my bone marrow in several places in my body.

The Lessons of Lymphoma

At first, my fear kept me from accepting the cancer diagnosis; it caught me off-guard. I couldn't believe I had cancer. I knew denial wouldn't help, so I chose to face the unknown head on. Searching the internet, I found

out more than enough information on both types of lymphoma and wished I hadn't gone there. The prognosis for
non-Hodgkin's lymphoma was not favorable. In fact, 63
percent of most non-Hodgkin's patients do not survive. I
chose to remain on the side of the positive. I decided to
stay around positive people, keep on exercising, and eat-
ing right. I saw myself as totally whole and healed from
cancer. I prayed I would be a good patient, I wanted to
learn whatever "lessons of lymphoma" God had planned
for me.

I started the first of eight cycles of chemotherapy and
came to fondly call it my chemo cocktail. Our family and
church chose to take the lighter side of things. We called
it tumor humor—the chemotherapy was cutting edge,
only on the market three years—made of mouse protein.
For fun, we made up mouse jokes. During the first treatment, I had developed a reaction to the medication. I told
the nurse, "I had this unusual craving to build a nest and
eat cheese." He said, "I think your tail was trying to grow
too fast." My sister-in-law even gave us a pair of Mickey
Mouse ears.

Many days I was exhausted or simply didn't feel well.
Verses such as Psalm 57:1 became very alive: "Have mercy
on me, O God, have mercy on me, for in you my soul takes
refuge. I will take refuge in the shadow of your wings until the disaster has passed." And "My heart and flesh may
fail, but God is the strength of my heart and my portion
forever." (Psalm 73:26 [NIV]).

God's Word and His people sustained me. Our loving
Sunday school class and church family made my time of
illness bearable. Paul developed a group email list, so not

only were people in Kern County praying, saints all across the world were, too. I received hundreds of encouraging phone calls. I cataloged binders full of emails and a dresser burgeoned with cards. Friends and family cooked endless lunches and dinners and sweet treats, did housecleaning and errand-running. We were graced with prayer quilts, flowers, plants, books, bracelets, and clothes.

Even during the midst of the deepest pain, side effects, anguish, and suffering, God was with me. I claimed promises like: "The God who gives life to the dead and calls things that are not as though they were" (Roman 4:17 [NIV]) and "He knows the way I take when he has tried me, I shall come forth as gold" (Job 23:10 [NIV]). Psalm 91:14 (NIV) became real: "Because she loves me, says the Lord, I will rescue her. I will protect her because she acknowledges my name. She will call upon me and I will answer her, I will be with her in trouble, I will deliver her and honor her. With long life will I satisfy her and show her my salvation."

The final PET scan came about two months after the final chemo treatment. I remember my doctor's excited voice on the other end of the phone: "Sheryl, the cancer is totally gone." I could hardly contain my joy. We made the announcement at church. I was elated God had chosen to lift me up again.

I had fallen flat on my face. This time it wasn't because of a night of drinking and drug use. I'd been face-down on the pavement spiritually, emotionally, and mentally because of an illness. God showed me favor. He extended His hand of healing and lifted me up again. I was cancer free! This was a miracle—God had delivered me from stage-four cancer! He had seen fit to heal me. "If the Lord delights in a man's way, he makes his steps firm; though he stumble, he will not fall, for the Lord upholds him with his hand" (Psalm 37:23, 24 [NIV]). This good news had to be celebrated. My mother-in-law headed up a celebration service instead of a funeral. We chose to gather together to praise God for His healing power and encourage each other in the process.

A Second Chance

The nine months of tests and treatments gave me lots of time to read and write. I studied healings, including the story of the ten lepers in Luke 17. Leprosy is a devastating and ostracizing disease; the infected typically live quarantined in a leper community outside city walls. Jesus was traveling between Samaria and Galilee. On his way to Jerusalem, ten lepers came to him. Healing from leprosy meant restored health and status. The ten lepers stood at a distance and cried out to him: "Jesus, Master, have pity on us!" (Luke 17:13 [NIV]). All ten of the lepers obeyed Jesus and showed themselves to the priests. But there was only one, when he saw he was healed, came back, praising God in a loud voice. He threw himself at Jesus's feet and thanked Him.

I desired to be like that one leper who thanked God. He healed me from stage-four cancer. I wanted to thank God by surrendering my life to Him. I was willing to go where God might send me.

Several years later, Paul opened the door for me to travel with him and speak to leadership and women's conferences in Africa. I was amazed how open the African people were to hearing about identity in Christ, forgiveness, dependence on God, and healing from cancer. Unlike in America, healings are a big deal in Africa and other third-world countries. Perhaps it's because the African people need more faith than we do. Or maybe we can learn from them?

Caroline's Story

I shared the story of my healing from stage-four cancer on the first day of the Kitale, Kenya, women's conference. Within hours, the news spread to a small village a good distance away. Caroline, a young Kenyan wife and mother, had battled cervical cancer for years. Upon her release from the hospital, on the second day of the conference, Caroline said to her husband, "I have got to meet this woman who has been healed of cancer. Take me to her." Traveling the rugged, unyielding road, thick with diesel smoke and congested with traffic, and after a half-day's journey, the couple arrived, tired but anticipating great things. The women's ministry team gathered to pray for Caroline and her family. At the end of the prayer time, we celebrated together, filled with hope and anticipation that God would glorify Himself as His will would be done through Caroline's life.

I thank God for the second chance he gave me through restoring my physical health. It was a new life, a new beginning. My prayer each day is the prayer of Moses: "Teach me Lord, to number my days that I might present to you a heart of wisdom" (Psalm 90:12 [NIV]). Thankfully during my free-fall into facing a deadly disease, and during the days "my parachute" didn't open because of despair or depression, what a powerful lesson to remember that my parachute lines were tangled with other believers who believed *for* me. I was able to rely on the prayers of others, the faith of others, and, at times, like a soft landing in a hot air balloon ride, the winds of blessing from others who paved the road of healing for me.

Study Questions for Chapter 9: Flat on My Face

Describe a time you or a family member faced a deadly illness.

1. Explain your feelings during diagnosis, prognosis, and treatment.

2. Share one or two scriptures that ministered to you or to someone you love.

3. Expound on a new truth you learned through this lesson.

4. Illustrate how you plan to encourage someone you love who is discouraged because of health problems.

10

Rise and Shine

Lieutenant Chisov was a Soviet Air Force Lieutenant on an Ilyushin Il-4 bomber. In January 1942, German fighters attacked his bomber, forcing him to bail out at an altitude of approximately 22,000 feet. With the battle still raging around him, Lt. Chisov intentionally did not open his parachute, since he feared that he would be an easy target for the Germans. He planned on dropping below the level of the battle, and then, once he was out of sight of the German fighters, he would open his chute and land safely. However, he lost consciousness on the way down and was unable to pull the ripcord. Miraculously, he was not killed. He hit the edge of a snowy ravine at an estimated speed of somewhere between 120 and 150 mph, then slid, rolled, and plowed his way down to the bottom. He suffered spinal injuries and a broken pelvis yet, remarkably, dodged death. He was given a second chance with a new beginning.[1]

A Second Chance

For believers, near-death experiences can help realign our focus to what is important to God. If we regularly remind ourselves of our temporary status on this earth, we regain our perspective on eternity. God waits for us to turn from everything else and give Him our all. He longs for us to rest in His will, to allow ourselves to fall into His loving embrace and trust. Some of us may never have a close encounter such as surviving a misguided parachute malfunction in the midst of a flight training exercise or facing a calculative error in an afternoon of skydiving. But even hearing about someone else's close brush with the temperance of life has a way of showing us the brevity of our existence. "Show me, O Lord, my life's end and the number of my days; let me know how fleeting is my life. You have made my days a mere handbreadth; and the span of my years is as nothing before you" (Psalm 39:5 [NIV]).

My survival from stage-four cancer realigned my every life decision. I was focused on the purpose of my ministry; I was so glad to be alive! I wanted my life to count for God. The year of the diagnosis of the disease, I'd been in negotiations with the radio station about a job promoting the ministry of the radio station. Understandably, when I was diagnosed and began chemotherapy treatments, our talks for my future employment with them were put on hold. Anxious to share how God had healed me from cancer and more, I believed working in Christian radio could only magnify those opportunities.

A few months after I received my clean bill of health, I reentered discussions with the radio station about a part-time position. There were a few meetings, emailed proposals, and a lot of prayer. Soon, I began my new job.

The radio station job gave me exposure to businesses and church partners. I enjoyed time in the community meeting with ministries that served the poor, homeless, needy, and got a firsthand look at what God was doing all over the county. One of my first assignments was to meet with business partners to thank them for their financial involvement and commitment to the radio ministry. Opportunities to minister were frequent. Once I met with a business leader going through a difficult court case, overwhelmed with accusations from a disgruntled client, who asked me for prayer. We shared a heart-connection, encouragement, and even a few tears.

Speaking invitations came to me from local churches, women's groups, and other support groups to share about my cancer-survival experience. I was excited to talk about how God had galvanized my faith, but more than that, to share with others that the same opportunity to trust waits for them. So many have head knowledge about God's power, but few truly have heart application. My exposure to the Africans' reliance and belief in God's healing power revealed the shallowness of my faith. I continued to process my response to my healing and chose to daily pray the prayer of Moses: "Teach me to number my days, that I might present to you a heart of wisdom" (Psalm 90:12 [NIV]). I remembered the lesson of the leper: "One of them, when he saw he was healed, came back, praising God in a loud voice. He threw himself at Jesus's feet and thanked him" (Luke 17:15 [NIV]). Each day, eagerly, I fell flat on my face in adoration, worship, and commitment to God's plan for my future.

A New Chapter

Paul and my marriage grew focused; Sarah relocated several states away to be closer to her boyfriend, and Ben moved to attend college out of town. Now we were empty-nesters. I looked forward to traveling with Paul for mission trips to Africa or wherever God would lead. However, I wasn't prepared for the day Paul came to me and said, "It's time for us to move on from this ministry." Paul had grown increasingly restless in his pastoral position at our church. When he first began the job, there was openness in the leadership about missions, and now it seemed the church was going in a different direction. Paul felt his time there had drawn to a close. He gave a two-month notice, and we began our long good-bye.

In the weeks that followed Paul's resignation announcement to the church body, I reluctantly processed the departure from *another* church family I had grown to love. I wasn't quite sure if this was God's timing or Paul's midlife crisis. I wondered where we would end up. We made plans to find another pastorate, sent out résumés and were even open to relocating out of town—wherever God might give us an opportunity to serve. We posted Paul's résumé online, so it was marketed across the nation. When he interviewed, we were confident that God would direct and guide us as long as we continued to let Him do the leading. Excited about the future, we both felt the urgency of the near-death cancer experience, which fueled our job search. Our small group study in Brennan Manning's *Abba's Child* showed us exactly where God wanted our focus: "Without deliberate awareness of the present risenness of Jesus, life is nonsense, all activity is useless, all relationships in vain. Apart from the risen Christ we live in a world of impenetrable mystery and utter obscurity—a world without meaning, a world of shifting phenomena, a world of death, danger, and darkness. A world of inexplicable futility. Nothing is interconnected. Nothing is worth doing, for nothing endures. The dark riddle of life is illuminated in Jesus; the meaning, purpose and goal of everything that happens to us and the way to make it all count can be learned only from the Way, the Truth and the Life."[2]

Even the in-limbo job search process had meaning. Each time Paul interviewed he shared God's plan and persistence for reaching the nations. It became increasingly evident a job at a church wouldn't completely fulfill God's purposes for his life nor would it satisfy Paul's desire for taking risks. For a few years, Paul had served on the board of International Christian Ministries (ICM), working with leaders in Africa and the Middle East. Plus his last four trips to Africa were under the umbrella of ICM, so it was a natural fit when the president approached him about coming on staff.

Because He Lives

Paul's job with ICM was perfect for him and an adjustment for me, since I was so used to working together with him in the church setting. But I knew I'd find a way to co-minister. Although I was used to my role as a pastor's wife, I was learning how to come alongside Paul as a missionary wife. We thoroughly enjoyed the work, especially the staff and international contributions to how God was working in Africa. We forged forward to fulfill demands and meet deadlines, excited about what was ahead.

Paul and I tried to overlap with each other in our ministries and involvements as often as possible, so when I was invited to speak at a local retreat center only forty-five minutes from our home, we were eager for the opportunity for him to join me. I was speaking just for the day. I drove to the center early on a Saturday morning. The retreat was finished by early afternoon. I called Paul to ask if he still wanted to ride his motorcycle up to visit, and he said, "Yes, I'm on my way." The retreat hostess had reserved a room for me, since the trip would take Paul at least an hour. I decided to take a nap. Little did I realize how much I would need this time to rest.

I heard the pipes of Paul's motorcycle announce his arrival minutes before he pulled into the retreat center. I walked down the path to meet him, thrilled about his presence. *He is so handsome,* I thought. *I am so blessed and proud to have Pastor Paul as my husband and life partner.* We walked around the retreat center for a couple of hours, making plans for future men's events or women's weekends and took pictures of each other by the vivid maroon bougainvillea before we departed. I got in my car. Paul's bike was parked behind me. I heard him start his engine, and, in a split second, he pulled around me, and, in a few more seconds he was out of sight. Soon after, I rounded a curve in the road and didn't see him. *He should have been right in front of me*, I thought. I looked to the left and saw a motorcycle turned on its side. I did a double take: *That was Paul's bike.* I turned my car around and pulled up next to the crumpled metal that was once Paul's perfect motorcycle. *But where was Paul?* Frantically, my eyes scanned the road and then rested on Paul's body face down in the weeds on the other side of the fence. I noticed he was heaving up and down. He was still breathing, much to my relief. Running to him, I asked, "What happened?" There was no response. I fumbled for my cell phone to call for help. The phone had no reception. I ran to a nearby cabin. No one was home. I stood on the side of the road trying to flag down anyone who drove by, frantically waving my hands in the air and yelling, "Help! My husband had an accident. Help me!" In anguish, I stood over my husband, best friend, life partner, and desperately prayed, "God, help him. Heal him. Lord God, help me!"

As if out of nowhere, a few locals came to help. Soon after, the fire department arrived, rolled Paul over, and began to assess his injuries. They told me he had a broken arm, several cracked ribs, a fractured left femur, and trouble breathing. The firemen assured me help was on the way—Paul would need to be airlifted to an emergency trauma unit. When the emergency medical technicians arrived by helicopter, I could see the concern in their distressed faces. No one would tell me the seriousness of Paul's injuries. I knew they were life-threatening.

I watched the helicopter disappear from view, as they took Paul to the trauma unit. I was overwhelmed. Just an hour before, I was strolling hand in hand with my beloved Paul. In a split second, everything changed. I had taught

Jeremiah 29:11–12 just a few hours before the accident, but now I was in a living nightmare. *Is this God's plan for me and for my future?* These were plans I had not approved. As I tearfully drove to the hospital, terrified by the unknown, I mentally reviewed the comforting scripture, "Plans to prosper you and not to harm you; plans to give you a hope and a future."

These words of comfort washed over my mind. Arriving at the hospital, I demanded to see Paul. My request rattled the receptionist. At once, I knew Paul was gone. I was whisked away into a curtained waiting room, where a couple of doctors strained to give me the dreaded news. "Paul didn't make it. He had a heart attack in the helicopter. The EMTs used the paddles on him and he did not survive. Paul has died."

"No!" I screamed. "There must be some mistake. It can't be true." The doctors assured me. It was true. Paul, my precious Paul was dead. It didn't make sense.

"Plans to prosper you and not to harm you; plans to give you a hope and a future" (Jeremiah 29:11,12 [NIV]).

How could Paul's death give me hope and a future? I remembered a prayer Beth Moore had taught us at a women's conference, a prayer she prayed for her family. I had prayed the same prayer for my family for about six weeks. It was a simple prayer that changed my life: "Lord, protect my family from everything but your glory." Paul's death would bring God glory.

I had to accept the reality of Paul going home early for my children and myself. Especially during the next week, as I called relatives to tell them of Paul's death, planned my beloved's funeral, and picked out a casket. I had to believe that although my world had turned upside down, God's love wouldn't change. I had to trust God's plan, even for Paul's untimely, unwelcome, and unfair death. I stood on Jeremiah 29:11,12 to find: "the plans that God would bring into my life not to harm me but to prosper me." (NIV) I chose to live in Christ's life, deciding to talk openly about Paul's death as something that God would use for His glory.

The day after Paul died, a dear friend and grief specialist, Dr. H. Norman Wright, stopped by my home to bring resources to help us through the process of assimilating our death blow. Thankfully, he brought multiple copies of his book, *Experiencing Grief*. That night, I couldn't sleep, so I picked up the little book and read it cover to cover in about an hour. This definition of grief stuck out to me: "Grief is the state we're in when we've lost a loved one. It's an inward look. You've been called into the house of mourning. It's not a comfortable place. It's not where you want to reside, but for a time, longer than you wish, you will. Often it will hurt, confuse, upset, and frighten you. It's described as intense emotional suffering or even acute sorrow."[3]

Paul and our ministry had touched many hearts and homes in our county for over twenty-five years. Radio listeners and past audiences from my speaking engagements and international travel sent e-mails, cards, and flowers. As in my season of cancer, once again the body of Christ came through. Many people wanted to *do* something; most people couldn't *do* anything to help us. We were devastated and traumatized by our grief. It's only because Jesus lives, I can face tomorrow.

The body of Christ kept praying. Our family was on the prayer list, and many hearts were broken by the loss of our precious Pastor Paul. One day a book arrived in the mail called *Come Away My Beloved*[4] by Francis J. Roberts. Each morning I felt as though I was seated in Jesus's lap, with His arms of comfort around me, allowing Him to minister to me during times I couldn't even function. Especially notable was: "Your Life Is a Weaving" — "My child, your life is a weaving. You may never know why certain experiences come. It is enough that My hand brings them all. My grace is not limited by sorrow and difficulty. Indeed, it shines like a strand of gold mixed in with the black of grief. My hand moves with infinite love, and I am creating a pattern of intricate beauty. Never be dismayed. The end will bring rejoicing for both yourself and Me. For you are My workmanship, created in Christ, even in His mind before the worlds existed. Doubt not, for My will shall be done."

I joined a Grief Share[5] group soon after and found others who knew how I felt. There were many encouraging quotes from the video teachings and *GriefShare* book such as, "Grief is the price you pay for loving someone. If there were no love, there would be no grief." I journaled and found solace in Christian music with extended times for prayer. I allowed God to heal my broken heart. It began to feel like the emotional bleeding was cauterized by His Word when I found verses such as Isaiah 57:1–2, "The righteous pass away, the godly often die before their time. No one seems to care or wonder why. No one seems to understand that God is protecting them from the evil to come. For the godly who die will rest in peace" (NIV). This gave me comfort that I knew I would see Paul again, and his soul was at rest.

Hope Again

Another resource that helped me get back up after Paul's death was the *One Year Book of Hope*.[6] Nancy Guthrie lost two children due to a genetic illness. Her expertise for encouraging the grieving process is extraordinary. This quote from one of the devotionals guided me through the difficult days of birthdays, anniversaries, and holidays: "What does God want to do in you or through you that would have to cost you this much?" Nancy asked, "Have you come to the place where you believe the glory of God is worth what it has cost you or will cost you in the future? Have you embraced the foundational truth that your life is not about you and your pain, but that you exist to display and enjoy the glory of God?" Then I realized letting go of Paul and the life we had together was not about me. It is all about God's glory. As I continue to share my story for God's glory, I ask Him each day to help me get back up so I can fulfill the plans and purposes He has for me.

Hillary's Story

Hillary heard the missions presentation I made at her home church about Pastor Paul's influence in my life and our connection there as a pastoral couple. I felt compelled to tell my story and honor Paul in his death; many in the audience had been part of our lives during our time of ministry there. Hillary's husband had succumbed to a yearlong battle with cancer just weeks before I spoke. After the service, Hillary approached me and said:

"I almost didn't come today. But I am so glad I did. Your story encouraged me to keep on going. I miss my husband so much, I can hardly stand it. But knowing that you have made it through gives me hope that I can make it, too. I am so thankful I am not alone in the journey. Thank you for your honesty. Thank you for restoring my hope."

Hillary's story is not unique. Those of us who walk the road of grieving the loss of a loved one want to know we are not alone. We want to know our loved one will not be forgotten. We want to know God can be trusted with our pain. "We suffer because of love. God whispers to us in our grief and shouts to us in our pain. Pain is God's megaphone to rouse a deaf world."[7] When we embrace the truth that our pain is not about us, that it is about God's glory, we can allow Romans 15:13 (NIV) to infuse everything we think, say, and do: "May the God of hope fill you with all joy and peace as you trust in Him, so that you may overflow with hope by the power of the Holy Spirit."

Whatever it is that God wants to do in you or through you that would have to cost you this much, surely it will be glorious!

Study Questions for
Chapter 10: Rise and Shine

1. Describe a time you have had to let go of a loved one due to death.

2. Share emotions (faces of grief) you felt during the time.

3. Expound on new thoughts you have from this chapter.

4. Explain how you feel God wants you to apply new truth to your life.

5. How do you expect God to help you get back up?

Endnotes

Chapter 1

1. Wiki How To Manual, www.wikipedia.org, 2001.

2. Brennan Manning, *Souvenirs of Solitude*, (Colorado Springs, CO: Navpress, 2009), 22.

3. St. Augustine of Hippo, *The Confessions of St. Augustine*, translated by John K. Ryan, (Catholic Company, 2000).

4. Webster's Dictionary, (Philippines: G & C Merriman, 1973).

5. Brennan Manning, *Abba's Child*, (Colorado Springs, CO: Navpress, 2002), 22.

6. John Eagan, *A Traveler Toward the Dawn*, *Abba's Child* (Colorado Springs, CO: Navpress, 2002), 5.

Chapter 2

1. The Free Fall Research Page (Marshfield, MA: Green Harbor Publications, 2001).

2. Nancy Leigh De Moss, *Lies Women Believe*, (Chicago, IL: Zondervan, 2001), 27.

3. Webster's Dictionary, (Philippines: G & C Merriman, 1973).

4. Neil Anderson, *The Bondage Breaker* (Eugene, OR: Harvest House, 2000), 46.

5. Francis McNutt, *Abba's Child* (Colorado Springs, CO: Navpress, 2002), 515.

6. Robb Thompson, *Wisdom Lessons for Living* (Winning in Life, 2007), 131.

7. Henrietta Mears, *Gospel Light* (Ventura, CA: Gospel Light).

8. Neil Anderson, *The Bondage Breaker* (Eugene, OR: Harvest House, 2000), 35.

Chapter 3

1. The Free Fall Research Page (Marshfield, MA: Green Harbor Publications, 2001).

2. Karen Scalf Linamen, *Just Hand Over the Chocolate and No One will Get Hurt* (Grand Rapids, MI: Revell, 1999).

3. Max Lucado, *UpWords Radio Show* (www.MaxLucado.com, 1-800-822-WORD).

4. Evagrius Ponticus, *A Daybook of Prayer* (Nashville, TN: Integrity House, 2001).

5. Martin Luther King, Jr, www.Quotes.com.

6. Neil Anderson, *Bondage Breaker* (Eugene, OR: Harvest House, 2000), 67.

7. Neil Anderson, *The Steps to Freedom* (Eugene, OR: Harvest House, 2000), 10.

8. Neil Anderson, *Bondage Breaker* (Eugene, OR: Harvest House, 2000), 75.

Chapter 4

1. *Guinness Book of World Records*, USA: 2012 (New York, NY: Bantam Books Mass-Marketing edition).

2. Fern Nichols, *Mom's In Touch Leader's Guide* (Poway, CA: Moms in Prayer International, 2000), http://www.momsintouch.org/.

Chapter 5

1. The Free Fall Research Page (Marshfield, MA: Green Harbor Publications, 2001).

2. Glenn Stanton, *Do All Marriages End in Divorce?* (Colorado Springs, CO: Focus on the Family, 2012), www.CitizenLink.com.

3. Webster's Dictionary, (Philippines: G & C Merriman, 1973).

4. John Bradshaw, *Home Coming* (New York/Toronto: Bantam Books, 1990), 8.

5. Steve Cooper, *The Legacy of the Father's Love: Loss and Abandonment Issues* (Indianapolis, IN: Family Tree Counseling Associates, 2011), www.FamilyTreeCounseling.com.

6. *Parent's Magazine*, Roper-Starch Survey, 2000.

Chapter 6

1. The Free Fall Research Page (Marshfield, MA: Green Harbor Publications, 2001).

2. Craig Smith, *Wives of Pastors often Struggle with Loneliness* (Grand Rapids, MI: TribLIVE, September, 2009).

Chapter 7

1. The Free Fall Research Page (Marshfield, MA: Green Harbor Publications, 2001).

2. Jill Briscoe, *Renewal on the Run, Encouragement for Wives Who Are Partners in Ministry* (Madison, WI: Harold Shaw, July 1992).

3. Beth Moore, *Get out of the Pit: Straight Talk on God's Deliverance* (Nashville, TN: Thomas Nelson, 2009).

4. H. Norman Wright, *Recovering from the Losses in Life* (Eugene, OR: Harvest House, 2007).

Chapter 8

1. The Free Fall Research Page (Marshfield, MA: Green Harbor Publications, 2001).

2. Tim Davis, *Pureheart Ministries* (Portland, OR: Pureheart Ministries, 2001).

Chapter 9

1. The Free Fall Research Page (Marshfield, MA: Green Harbor Publications, 2001).

2. David Jeremiah, *A Bend in the Road* (Nashville, TN: W Publishing Group, a division of Thomas Nelson, 2000), 45.

3. C. S. Lewis, *A Grief Observed* (New York, NY: HarperCollins Publishers, 1961), 85.

Chapter 10

1. The Free Fall Research Page (Marshfield, MA: Green Harbor Publications, 2001).

2. Brennan Manning, *Abba's Child* (Colorado Springs, CO: Navpress, 2002), 107.

3. H. Norman Wright, *Experiencing Grief* (Nashville, TN: B & H Publishing Group, 2004), 3.

4. Frances J. Roberts, *Come Away My Beloved* (Urichsville, OH: Barbour Publishing, Inc., 2002), 229.

5. Grief Share, (Wake Forest, NC: Church Initiative, 2008), www.griefshare.org.

6. Nancy Guthrie, *The One Year Book of Hope* (Eugene, OR: Harvest House Publishers, 2004), 167.

7. *Shadowlands*, the biographical movie of the life of C.S. Lewis, directed by Richard Attenborough in 1993 (HBO Home Video, 1993).

God Thoughts: Experiencing Him by His Names

Have you ever felt like God doesn't care or isn't there? Our awareness of God influences actions, motives, attitudes and desires. *God Thoughts: Experiencing Him by His Names* will help you to know, understand, and practice the presence of God in your daily life. Observing just one name of God is like looking at a postcard of the Grand Canyon. It shows an undersized segment of a breathtaking view. Absorbing truth about God by studying just one of His names at a time, we can better understand the reality and certainty of His character and experience the power of His presence in our daily lives. As we search to comprehend His names, we grasp His commitment to us and are open to His purposes for our lives. God is there and He does care. In fact, God has big plans for you! "What is His name and the name of His Son? Tell me if you know!" Proverbs 30:4b (NIV)

God Thoughts: Experiencing Him By His Names is a resource for personal use. The book can be used for small group studies, weekly women's Bible study, or as a guide for a sermon series. Readers of *God Thoughts: Experiencing Him by His Names* will:

- Understand thirty-one of God's names
- Experience God's power in fresh ways
- Explain thirty-one of God's names to others
- Desire to know more about God
- Apply their experience of God to other areas of life – parenting, marriage, marketplace, and personal communication

God Thoughts: Experiencing Him by His Names is divided into four distinct parts:

1. **Introduction.** The book, *God Thoughts: Experiencing Him by His Names* is a way to know God through understanding His names. By investigating the names of God one at a time, we look at snapshots of His vast and complex personality. The names of God each reveal something about His character, His purposes and His commitment to us and give handles to life applications. Exodus 20:24 (NIV) says, "Wherever I cause My name to be honored, I will come to you and bless you." God wants us to understand Him as we study His character through His names.

2. **Prayer of Thanksgiving.** To God, for the opportunity to get to know Him by studying His names.

3. **Master Plan of Growth.** Three essential components will be taught to encourage spiritual growth:Worship, Bible study and prayer.

4. **Contract of Agreement.** For any habit that prospers us, consistency and practice make a difference. Beginning a new habit for an intentional thirty-one day increment of time makes success not only possible but also highly probable. The reader will commit to learn about God, to study His names daily, with fifteen minutes of prayer and fifteen minutes of Bible study.

About the Author

"Exchanging hurt for hope," is Sheryl Giesbrecht's focus. She is a radio personality, author, and speaker. A pastor's wife for over twenty-eight years, mother of two adult children, cancer survivor, and widow, she is passionate about sharing how God takes the ashes of our losses, bitterness, and mistakes; and turns them into something remarkably beautiful.

Sheryl is a dynamic teacher and motivating leader who has equipped hundreds and facilitated the training of thousands of leaders in the United States and internationally. Sheryl's own story began with her conversion to Christ over thirty years ago. Once a rebellious teenager, alcoholic, and drug addict, Sheryl knows what it is to overcome physical addictions.

In ministry and leadership, Sheryl has endured changes and challenges, moving her to a deep faith, trust, and dependence on God. Healed of stage 4 lymphoma, Sheryl knows the heartbreak of disappointment, discouragement, and disease. Recently widowed, Sheryl has walked through the valley of the shadow of death. From the depths of these experiences, her desire is for believers to be set free from past hurts, to be healed and whole emotionally.

As Focus on the Family's columnist for Pastor's Wives for four years, Sheryl's audio interview with H. B. London on the topic, "Success in Ministry, Call to Ministry," continues to be offered through Focus on the Family's Pastor's Family Resources. Hundreds of her columns, magazine and devotional articles have appeared in *Focus on the Family Magazine*, *Just Between Us*, *Discipleship Journal*, *Contemporary Christian Music*, Walk Thru the Bible's - *InDeed* and *Tapestry* publications.

Sheryl's radio show, *Kindred Moments*, can be heard each weekday evening and Sunday afternoons on KAXL 88.3 FM Music for Life (www.KAXL.com). Her nationally syndicated radio show, *Turn up the Music with Sheryl Giesbrecht*, is heard on numerous networks across the United States. (www.KERN.com). Sheryl is avid about reaching out to the poor and needy, locally through the Rescue Mission and world-wide through Compassion International.

Sheryl is the Executive Director of International Christian Ministries (ICM), which trained over two million African leaders in 2008. Sheryl carries the baton, mobilizing believers to come alongside to facilitate training African and Middle Eastern pastors and leaders as it was passed to her by her late husband, Paul, former vice president of international operations with ICM. She is a sought-after international speaker, offering the hope and healing only found in the Lord Jesus Christ. (www.ICMUSA.org)

The joys of Sheryl's life are her two children, son-in-law and daughter-in-law, plus memories of her beloved husband. Sheryl holds a bachelor of arts from Biola University, a master's in ministry, and a doctorate of theology.

www.kaxl.com * www.ICMUSA.org * wwwFromAshesToBeauty.com

To Contact Sheryl:
Facebook/Scribd: Sheryl Giesbrecht
Twitter: #SGiesbrecht
Blog: Sheryl's Blog
To schedule Sheryl for your retreat, conference or event:
www.SpeakUpSpeakerServices.com